P9-ART-621

THE POWER OF A *Praying®* *Woman*

STORMIE OMARTIAN

HARVEST HOUSE™ PUBLISHERS
EUGENE, OREGON

Unless otherwise indicated, Scripture verses are taken from the New King James Version. Copyright © 1982 by Thomas Nelson, Inc. Used by permission. All rights reserved.

Verses marked NLT are taken from the *Holy Bible*, New Living Translation, copyright ©1996. Used by permission of Tyndale House Publishers, Inc., Wheaton, Illinois 60189, U.S.A. All rights reserved.

Verses marked ASV are taken from the American Standard Version of the Bible.

All the stories related in this book are true, but most of the names have been changed to protect the privacy of the people mentioned.

Cover by Koechel Peterson & Associates, Minneapolis, Minnesota

THE POWER OF A PRAYING® WOMAN
Copyright © 2002 By Stormie Omartian
Published by Harvest House Publishers
Eugene, Oregon 97402

Library of Congress Cataloging-in-Publication Data

Omartian, Stormie.
The power of a praying woman / Stormie Omartian.
p. cm.
Includes bibliographical references.
ISBN 0-7369-0974-5 (Deluxe Edition)
ISBN 0-7369-0855-2 (Trade Edition)
1. Christian women—Religious life. 2. Prayer—Christianity. I. Title.
BV4527 .0435 2002
248.8' 43—dc21 2002006077

Printed in the United States of America.

02 03 04 05 06 07 08 09 10 11 / IP-KB / 10 9 8 7 6 5 4 3 2 1

This book is dedicated to my sisters in Christ all over the world who long to deepen their walk with the Lord, move into everything God has for them, and become all He made them to be.

Acknowledgments

With special thanks:

To Susan Martinez, for your prayer support and hard work as my secretary, assistant, prayer partner, and friend.

To my husband, Michael, for your love, prayers, and good cooking.

To my children, for simply living.

To my faithful prayer partners.

To Pastor Jack Hayford, Pastor Rice Broocks, Pastor Tim Johnson, Pastor Ray McCollum, Pastor John Roher, Pastor Jim Laffoon, and Pastor Scott Bauer, for your life-saving prayers and life-changing words.

To my Harvest House family—Bob Hawkins Jr., Carolyn McCready, Terry Glaspey, Betty Fletcher, Julie McKinney, Teresa Evenson, LaRae Weikert, Kim Moore, and Peggy Wright—for all your encouragement and support.

To the thousands of women who have sent letters, e-mail, and faxes to me sharing your struggles, joys, longings, and the desires of your heart.

Contents

Let the beauty of the L*ORD* *our God be upon us,*
and establish the work of our hands for us.
PSALM 90:17

The Power

It doesn't matter what age you are, what your marital status is, what the condition of your body and soul is, or how long you have or have not been a believer—if you are a woman, this book is for you. I've been a devoted follower of the Lord for over 30 years and I have not fallen away from Him in all that time, yet I need this book too. In fact, I wrote it for myself as much as I wrote it for you. That's because I'm like you. Many days I find life difficult rather than easy, complex rather than simple, potentially dangerous rather than safe, and exhausting rather than exhilarating. Often it's more like a strong, hot, dry wind than it is a soft, cool, refreshing breeze.

But I have come to know that God can smooth my path, calm the storms, keep me and all I care about safe, and even make my way simple when I ask Him to carry the complexities of life for me. But these things don't just happen. Not without prayer.

In the midst of our busy lives, too often we don't pray enough. Or we only pray about the most pressing issues and neglect to take the time to really get close to God, to know Him better, and to share with Him the deepest longings of our heart. In our pray-and-run existence, we shut off the very avenue by which He brings blessings into our lives. And we risk waking up one day with that empty, insecure feeling in the pit of our stomach frightening us with the thought that our foundation may be turning into sand and our protective armor may be becoming as fragile as an eggshell. This is what happened to me.

A few years ago, I had become so busy with working, taking care of teenagers, trying to be a good wife, running a home, writing books and traveling to promote them, being at all church meetings, helping people who needed it, and trying to make everyone happy, that I neglected the most important thing—my intimate walk with God. It's not that I stopped walking with Him. To the contrary, I couldn't make it through a day without Him. It's not that I stopped praying. Actually, I was praying more than ever about everyone else on the planet. But I didn't pray about my own walk with Him. It's not that I didn't read His Word. I read for hours as I did research in the Scriptures for different projects I was working on and the Bible study classes I was taking. But I didn't give God time to speak to me personally through it. I was busy doing good and neglected to do what was best. I became Martha instead of Mary without even realizing it (Luke 10:38-42).

I didn't take enough time for God and me alone, and as a result I became so depleted I couldn't go on. I felt like that eggshell, as if I could be crushed with very little outside pressure. I knew I needed more of God in my life, and nothing on earth was more important than that. There wasn't anything else that could satisfy the hunger I felt inside except more of His presence. And I came to realize how important it was for me to guard and protect my personal relationship with God in prayer.

The way to avoid the kind of thing I experienced is to pray about every aspect of our life in such a manner that it will keep us spiritually anchored and reminded of what God's promises are to us. It will keep us focused on who God is and who He made us to be. It will help us live God's way and not our own. It will lift our eyes from the temporal to the eternal and show us what is really important. It will give us the ability to distinguish the truth from a lie. It will strengthen our faith and encourage us to believe for the impossible. It will enable us to become the women of God we *long* to be and believe we *can* be. Who among us doesn't need that?

In my previous books on prayer, I have shared the ways husbands and wives can pray for one another, parents can pray for their children, and people can pray for their nation. In this book, I want to share how *you* can pray for *YOU*. I want to help you draw close to your heavenly Father, to feel His arms around you, to maintain a right heart before Him, to live in the confidence of knowing you are in the center of His will, to discover more fully who He made you to be, to find wholeness and completeness in Him, and to move into all He has for you. In other words, I want to show you how to effectively cover your life in prayer so that you can have more of God in your life.

Why Is It so Hard to Pray for Myself?

Do you find it is easier to pray for other people than it is to pray for yourself? I know I do. I can pray for my husband, my children, other family members, acquaintances, friends, and people I've never even met whom I hear about in the news far easier than I can pray for my own needs. For one thing, their needs are easy for me to identify. Mine are numerous, sometimes complicated, often difficult to determine, and certainly not easy to label. We women know what we *think* we need most of the time. We are able to recognize the obvious. But we are often too emotionally involved in the people around us and the day-to-day existence of our lives to be able to figure out how we should be praying for ourselves beyond the immediate and urgent. Sometimes we can be so overwhelmed by our circumstances that our prayer is simply a basic cry for help.

Do you ever have times when your life seems out of control? Do you ever feel pressured, as if your days are so busy that you fear you're missing out on a certain quality of life because of it? Do you worry that you are neglecting one or more areas of your life because you are trying to fill numerous roles and meet many expectations? I've experienced that too.

Have you ever felt as if your life is stuck in one place and you're going nowhere? Or worse yet, you are going backward? Have you had times when you've lost your vision for the future? Or have you never really had one to begin with? Have you wondered whether you can actually move into the full purpose and destiny God has for you? Have you experienced feelings of emptiness, frustration, or unfulfillment? I, too, have felt all those things.

Do you hunger for a greater sense of the Lord's presence in your life? Do you desire to know God in a deeper way? Do you want to serve Him better and more completely but don't feel you have the time, energy, or opportunity to do so? Do you need to spend more time with Him in prayer? Do you want your prayers to be accompanied by greater faith so that you can see greater answers to them? Do you need a more complete knowledge and understanding of God's Word? Do you ever just long to throw your arms wide open and embrace Jesus, white robes and all, and feel His embrace of you? So do I.

The good news is that this is the way God *wants* you to feel.

God wants you to long for *His* presence. He wants you to find your fulfillment in *Him* and nothing else. He wants you to walk closely with *Him*. He wants you to increase in faith and knowledge of *His* Word. He wants you to put all your hopes and dreams in *His* hands and look to *Him* to meet all of your needs. When you do, *He* will open the storehouse of blessing upon your life. That's because these things are *His* will for you.

But none of this happens without prayer.

Where Do I Go to Get My Needs Met?

Every woman has needs. But many of us are guilty of looking to other people to meet them—especially the men in our lives. Too often we expect *them* to meet the needs that only *God* can fill. And then we are disappointed when they can't. We expect too much from *them* when our expectations should be in *God*.

My friend Lisa Bevere expressed it best when she said that for centuries women have "wrestled and waged war with the sons of Adam in an attempt to get them to bless us and affirm our value. But this struggle has left us frustrated at best....In the end, it is all a senseless and exhausting process in which both parties lose. It is not the fault of the sons of Adam; they cannot give us the blessing we seek, and we have frightened them by giving them so much power over our souls. We must learn that the blessings we truly need come only from God."*

---

* Lisa Bevere, *Kissed the Girls and Made Them Cry*, (Nashville: Tommy Nelson, 2002), pp 189-90.

We will never be happy until we make *God* the source of our fulfillment and the answer to our longings. He is the *only* one who should have power over our souls.

We have to put our expectations in the Lord and not in other things or people. I know this is easier said than done. So let's start with the easy part. Let's say to God, "Lord, I look to You for everything I need in my life. Help me to put all my expectations in You." And whenever you are disappointed because your needs are not being met, talk to yourself and say, "My soul, wait silently for God alone, for my expectation is from Him" (Psalm 62:5). Then tell God about all your needs and everything that is in your heart. Don't worry, He won't be surprised or shocked. He already knows. He is just waiting to hear it from you.

More Than Just a Survivor

If you're like me, you don't want to live the kind of life where you are barely hanging on. You don't want to merely eke out an existence, find a way to cope with your misery, or just get by. You want to have the abundant life Jesus spoke of when He said, "I have come that they may have life, and that they may have it more abundantly" (John 10:10).

We don't want to be women who hear the truth but seldom act in faith to appropriate it for our lives. We don't want to be forever grappling with doubt, fear, insecurity, and uncertainty. We want to live life *on* purpose and *with* purpose. We find it boring to live like a baby, feeding only on milk. We want the solid food of God's truth so we can grow into a life that is exciting and productive.

None of us enjoys going around in circles, always passing through the same territory and coming back to the same problems, same frustrations, same mistakes, and same limitations. We don't want to become calloused, hard-hearted, bitter, unforgiving, anxious, impatient, hopeless, or unteachable. We don't want to end up with a negative attitude that says, "My situation will never *be* any different because it hasn't *been* any different for a long time." We want to break out of any self-defeating cycle of repeated patterns and habits and be able to transcend ourselves, our limitations, and our circumstances. We want to be more than just a survivor.

We want to be an overcomer. We want to be a part of something greater than ourselves. We want to be connected to what God is doing on earth in a way that bears fruit for His kingdom. We want to have a sense of purpose in our lives. We want to abound in God's love and blessings. We want it all. All God has for us. But we can never achieve that quality of life outside the power of God. And then only as we pray.

How Do I Move in the Power of God?

We've all had times when we feel completely powerless in the face of our circumstances. We've proven to ourselves over and over that we don't have what it takes to attain any kind of permanent transformation in our lives. We know without a doubt that our best efforts to change ourselves or our circumstances in ways that are significant or lasting never work. We recognize our need for a power outside of and far greater than ourselves. But there is only one power in the world great enough to help us rise above ourselves and the difficult things we face. That is the power of God.

Without God's power, we can't transcend our limitations or get out of our rut. We can't stand strong in the face of all that opposes us. We are doomed to a life of spiritual mediocrity. Without the power of God's Holy Spirit working in us, we can't be liberated from everything that keeps us from moving into all God has for us.

We don't want to spend our lives waiting to be delivered from all that limits us and separates us from God's best. We want to be set free *now*. But that can't happen if we refuse to acknowledge the Holy Spirit's power. When we deny the Holy Spirit's attributes we become like those people the Bible speaks of who live "having a form of godliness but denying its power" (2 Timothy 3:5). We become professional Christians who talk "Christianese" with such a slick veneer of superficiality that it makes us untouchable and keeps us untouched. We become all show and no heart. All correctness and no love. All judgment and no mercy. All self-assurance and no humility. All talk and no tears. We live powerless and meaningless lives without any hope for real transformation. And without transformation, how can we ever rise above our limitations and be God's instrument to reach the world around us? And that is what life is all about.

God wants us to understand "what is the exceeding greatness of His power toward us who believe" (Ephesians 1:19). He wants us to know this power that raised Jesus "from the dead and seated Him at His right hand in the heavenly places, far above all principality and power and might and dominion, and every name that is named" (Ephesians 1:20-21). He wants us to understand that Jesus is not weak toward us, but mighty *in* us (2 Corinthians 13:3). He wants us to understand that "though He was crucified in weakness, yet He lives by the power of God," and even though we are also weak, we live by the power of God too (2 Corinthians 13:4). God wants us to see that "we have received, not the spirit of the world, but the Spirit who is from

God, that we might know the things that have been freely given to us by God" (1 Corinthians 2:12).

I can't make you see or cause you to comprehend the power of God or the way the Holy Spirit wants to work in you. That is beyond my capabilities and authority in your life. But you don't need me to convince you because the Holy Spirit will do that Himself. Jesus said, "the Helper, the Holy Spirit, whom the Father will send in My name, He will teach you all things" (John 14:26). But you first have to acknowledge the Holy Spirit and invite Him to move in you freely.

We can only move in the power of God's Spirit if we have first received Jesus as Savior. You need to "know the love of Christ which passes knowledge; that you may be filled with all the fullness of God" (Ephesians 3:19). When you have Jesus as ruler of your life, you will come to know Him as the one "who is able to do exceedingly abundantly above all that we ask or think, according to the power that works in us" (Ephesians 3:20). Because of His Holy Spirit in us—or His *power* in us—He can do more in our lives than we can even think to ask for. How great is that?

Being filled with the Holy Spirit is not something that happens against our will. It is something we have to be open to, something we must desire, something for which we have to ask. "If you then, being evil, know how to give good gifts to your children, how much more will your heavenly Father give the Holy Spirit to those who ask Him!" (Luke 11:13). We have a choice about whether we will be filled with the Holy Spirit or not. We have to ask God to do that.

I am not going to get into the various doctrines of men about the Holy Spirit of God. There seem to be as many of these as there are denominations. All I am asking is that you recognize the Holy Spirit of God as the *power* of God, and that you ask God to fill you with His Holy Spirit so He can empower you to move into all He has for you. The Bible says, "be filled with the Spirit" (Ephesians 5:18). Life works better when we do what the Bible says.

The Power to Become All God Made You to Be

Today, more and more believing women are being given an open door to become all they were created to be. They are moving out in different areas of expertise and ministry and making an important difference in the lives of those whom God puts in their realm of influence. They are learning to rely on the power of God to prepare them and open the doors. They are also realizing that they are not just an afterthought in the order of God's creation, but they were created for a special purpose. They might not know exactly what that purpose is or all that it entails, but they know that it is to do good for others and glorify God.

An important reason more women are rising up to fulfill the destiny God has for them is because men are rising up to their place of spiritual authority and leadership. This is an answer to the prayers of countless women and something for which we must praise God. Women need this spiritual covering. When it's done right—with strength, humility, kindness, respect, and understanding—and not with abuse, arrogance, self-promotion, cruelty, harshness, or lovelessness, it becomes a place of safety for a woman. Being in right order in our lives is something to be desired.

The Bible says that "the woman ought to have a symbol of authority on her head" (1 Corinthians 11:10). This means spiritual authority, and it is very important. *Everyone* is supposed to be submitted to divinely appointed authority It's part of God's order. God won't pour into our lives all He has for us until we are in right relationship with the proper authority figures whom He has placed in our lives. They are there for our protection and benefit. God's power is too precious and too powerful to be let loose in an unsubmitted soul. (This is something to *pray* about, not *worry* about, so we'll do that in chapter 9.)

God's Promises to You

So often we don't move into all God has for us because we don't understand what it *is* He has for us. We may know He has given many promises for our lives, but if we don't know *exactly* what these promises are, we can't get a clear perspective on our situation. God's "divine power has given to us all things that pertain to life and godliness, through the knowledge of Him who called us by glory and virtue, by which have been given to us exceedingly great and precious promises, that through these you may be partakers of the divine nature" (2 Peter 1:3-4).

We need to know these promises well enough to keep them perpetually in our minds and on our hearts. In fact, the *deeper* they are etched in our souls the better off we will be. That's because the enemy of our soul will try to steal them from us. He doesn't want us to know the truth about ourselves. So we must grab on to these promises with all our might. We must cling to them like life and refuse to let them go.

For this reason, at the end of each chapter in this book there is a section called "God's Promises to Me." In it I have listed important promises from God's Word that are applicable to that particular subject. I want us to declare these promises out loud in the face of all obstacles in order to erase any doubt about those priceless truths for our lives. As you read each one, determine what God's promise in that particular Scripture means specifically for you and your life.

In some instances, determine what promise is *implied* in that Scripture. Take for example the verse, "Watch and pray, lest you enter into temptation. The spirit indeed is willing, but the flesh is weak" (Matthew 26:41). The implied promise here is that if you pray and are watchful, you won't fall into temptation.

While most of God's promises are pleasant and positive, some are not because they are warnings to us. It's like saying to a child, "If you do *this*, there is this reward. But if you do *that*, I *promise* you there will be these unpleasant consequences." Because God keeps *all* of His promises, it's important to know them well.

Time to Move On

Although it may often feel like it, there is never a time when *nothing* is happening in your life. That's because whether you realize it or not, you are never standing still. You are either going forward or you're sliding back. You are either becoming *more* like Christ every day or you're becoming *less* like Him. There is no neutral position in the Lord. And that is the very reason I wrote this book. I want you and me to keep moving forward. I don't want us to wake up one morning and realize we never laid a good foundation in the things of God or we didn't protect the foundation we had with prayer. I want us to move forward by spending quality time with the Lover of our soul every day. I want us to become *passionate* about God. I want us to find out what we are supposed to be doing and then do it. This is not about getting things *from* God, although He has much He wants to give to us. It's about getting *into* God and allowing Him to get into *us*. It's about letting *Him* make us complete.

When we live this way, according to God's Word and by the power of His Holy Spirit, then we can trust that we are in the right place at the right time and that the Lord is working His perfect will in our lives. We can trust that He is moving us into the life of wholeness and blessing He has for us. Shall we get started?

My Prayer to God

Lord, You have said in Your Word that whoever believes in You will have rivers of living water flowing from their heart (John 7:38). I believe in You, and I long for Your living water to flow in and through me today and every day that I'm alive. I invite Your Holy Spirit to fill me afresh right now. Just as a spring is constantly being renewed with fresh water so that it stays pure, I ask You to renew me in that same way today.

Your Word says that "the Spirit also helps in our weaknesses. For we do not know what we should pray for as we ought, but the Spirit Himself makes intercession for us with groanings which cannot be uttered" (Romans 8:26). Lord, I realize I don't know how to pray as I need to, nor as often as I want to, but I invite You, Holy Spirit, to pray through me. Help me in my weakness. Teach me the things I don't know about You.

I am desperately aware of how much I need Your power to transform me and my circumstances. I don't want to live an ineffective life. I want to live in the dynamic power of Your Spirit. I don't want to be a spiritual underachiever. I want to be an overcomer. You paid a price for me so that I could be owned by You. Help me to live like it. You planned out a course for my life so that I could be defined by You. Help me to act like it. You made it possible for me to defeat my enemy. Help me not to forget it. You sent Your Holy Spirit so that I could live in power. Help me to fulfill that promise. You gave Your life for me because You loved me. Help me to do the same for You.

I put all my expectations in You, Lord. I repent of the times I have expected other people or other things to meet my needs when I should have been looking to You. I know that You are the only one who can complete me because You are everything I need. All that I have ever wanted in my life can be found in You. Help me to remember to live not in my own strength, but by the power of Your Spirit living in me. Forgive me for the times I have forgotten to do that. Enable me to grow in the things of Your kingdom so that I can become a whole, properly functioning, contributing, productive child of Yours who moves forward in Your purpose for my life.

God's Promises to Me

We have this treasure in earthen vessels,
that the excellence of the power may be of God and not of us.

2 Corinthians 4:7

The message of the cross is foolishness to those who are perishing, but to us who are being saved it is the power of God.

1 Corinthians 1:18

My grace is sufficient for you, for My strength is made perfect in weakness.
2 CORINTHIANS 12:9

God both raised up the Lord and will also raise us up by His power.
1 CORINTHIANS 6:14

When the Helper comes, whom I shall send to you from the Father, the Spirit of truth who proceeds from the Father, He will testify of Me.
JOHN 15:26

CHAPTER ONE

Lord, Draw Me into a Closer Walk with You

Before I came to know the Lord, I was involved in all kinds of occult practices and Eastern and New Age religions. I searched for God in each one of them, hoping to find some meaning or purpose for my life. I was desperate to find a way out of the emotional pain, fear, and depression I had experienced on a daily basis since I was a child. I thought there surely must be a God, and if I could just be good enough to get close to Him, perhaps something of His greatness would rub off on me, and then I could feel better about myself and my life.

Of course I was never able to do that because the gods I chased after were distant, cold, and remote. And this depressed me all the more because I was raised by a mother who was distant, cold, and remote, not to mention abusive, frightening, and cruel. It was later determined that she was mentally ill, and I have since forgiven her for all that I suffered at her hand. Nevertheless, the memories of my childhood eventually snowballed into an avalanche of pain that became so unbearable that I ended up being suffocated by my own hopelessness and crushed into suicidal despair.

But it was here at the lowest point in my life, when I was 28 years old, that I learned who God really is and received Jesus as my Savior. This began a process of deliverance, healing, and restoration, the likes of which I had never dreamed possible.

From the time I received the Lord and began to feel His life working *in* me, I could see the common thread in all those *other* religions and practices I had dabbled in previously. This similarity was that the gods of each of those religions had no power to save or transform a human life. But the God of the *Bible* did. *He* is the one, true, living God. And when we find *Him* and receive *Him*, His Spirit comes to dwell *in* us. By the power of His spirit, He transforms us from the inside out and miraculously changes our circumstances and our lives.

I also learned that He is a God who can be found. A God who can be known. A God who wants to be close to us. That's why He is called Immanuel, which means "God *with* us." But He draws close to *us* as we draw close to *Him* (James 4:8).

If I could sit down and talk with you in person about your life, I would tell you that if you have received the Lord, the answer to what you need is within you. That's because the Holy Spirit of God is within you, and He will lead you in all things and teach you everything you need to know. He will transform you and your circumstances beyond your wildest dreams if you will give up trying to do it on your own and let *Him* do it *His* way and in *His* time.

This is not about striving to be good enough to get to God, for there is no way any of us can be. This is about letting all of the goodness of God be *in* you. It's about drawing closer to God and sensing Him drawing closer to you. This is about an intimate walk with God and the wholeness that will be worked in you because of it.

I Know What You Want

I traveled all over the United States speaking to women's groups during three of the last four years. Nearly everywhere I went in that period of time, I took a survey for a book I was writing called *The Power of a Praying® Husband.* I wanted to know how women most wanted to be prayed for. Their response was not surprising, but the fact that it was unanimous in every city and every state was amazing. The number one personal need of all women surveyed was that they would grow spiritually and have a deep, strong, vital, life-changing, faith-filled walk with God. I eventually stopped taking the survey because the results were always the same. I got the point!

I'm sure that you, like me and many women, want a deep, intimate, loving relationship with God. You wouldn't be reading this book if you didn't. You long for the closeness, the connection, the affirmation that who you are is good and desirable. But God is the only one who can give all that to you all of the time. Your deepest needs and longing will only be met in an intimate relationship with Him. No person will ever reach as deeply into you as God will. No one can ever know you as well or love you as much. That insatiable longing for more that you feel, the emptiness you want those closest to you to fill, is put there by God so that *He* can fill it.

God wants us to want Him. And when we realize that it's Him that we want, we become free. We are free to identify the longings, loneliness, and emptiness inside of us as our signal that we need to draw near to God with open arms and ask Him to fill us with more of Himself. But this deep and intimate relationship with God that we all desire and can't live without doesn't just happen. It must be sought after, prayed for, nurtured, and treasured. And we must *continually* seek after, pray for, nurture, and treasure it.

Five Good Ways to Tell if Your Walk with God Is Shallow

1. *If you follow the Lord for only what He can do for you*, your walk with Him is shallow. If you love Him enough to ask Him what *you* can do for *Him*, then your relationship is growing deep.

2. *If you only pray to God when things are tough or you need something*, then your walk with Him is shallow. If you find yourself praying to Him many times a day just because you love to be in His presence, then your relationship is growing deep.

3. *If you get mad at God or disappointed in Him when He doesn't do what you want*, then your walk with Him is shallow. If you can praise God no matter what is going on in your life, then your relationship with Him is growing deep.

4. *If you love God only because of what He does*, then your walk with Him is shallow. If you love and reverence Him for who He *is*, then your relationship with Him is growing deep.

5. *If you think you have to beg God or twist His arm to get Him to answer your prayers*, then your walk with Him is shallow. If you believe that God wants to answer the prayers you pray in line with His will, then your relationship with Him is growing deep.

Spending Time Alone with Him

We can never draw close to God and get to know Him well, or develop the kind of intimate relationship we want, unless we spend time alone with Him. It's in those private times that we are refreshed, strengthened, and rejuvenated. It's then we can see our lives from God's perspective and discover what is really important. That's where we understand who it is we belong to and believe in.

God has so much to speak into your life. But if you don't draw apart from the busyness of your day and spend time alone with Him in quietness and solitude, you will not hear it. Jesus Himself spent much time alone with God. If anyone could get away with not doing it, surely it would have been Him. How much more important must it be for us?

I know finding time alone to pray can be difficult. Especially when the enemy of your soul doesn't want you to do that. But if you will make it a priority by setting a specific time to pray daily, perhaps writing it in your calendar the way you would any other important date, and determine to keep that standing appointment with God, you'll see answers to your prayers like never before.

Remember, if you haven't been praying much, you can't expect things to change overnight. It takes a while to get the enormous ocean liner of your life turned around and headed in a different direction. It doesn't immediately reposition itself the moment you begin steering. In fact, you may hardly see any changes at first. It's the same way with prayer. Prayer can turn your life around, but it doesn't always happen the moment you utter your first words. It may take a time of continued prayer before you actually see the scenery change. This is normal, so don't give up. You will soon be heading full speed in a new direction. Far too often people give up just before their breakthrough into the realm of answered prayer. Remember, this trip is not a mini-vacation tour around the harbor, it's a lifelong voyage to meet your destiny. Giving up is not an option.

Naming Names

Do you ever have trouble remembering names? I know I do. Especially when I meet a large number of people at one time. I can remember faces and names separately, but I don't always put the right ones together. And that can get me into trouble. With God it's a different situation. He has only one face, but many, many names. But if we don't know all of His names, we may not understand all the aspects of His character.

God has literally hundreds of names. Sometimes, though, it seems we often have trouble just remembering a few of the basic ones. We may forget one just when we need to remember it. For example, we may think of God as our heavenly *Father*, but forget that He is also our *Husband* and *Friend*. Or we may remember Him as our *Comforter*, but forget that He is our *Deliverer*. We might think of Him as our *Protector*, but fail to remember Him as our *Healer*. Some people never think of God beyond being their Savior, which in itself is more than we deserve. But God wants to be even more than that to us. He wants us to know all the aspects of His character because the way we recognize God will affect the way we live our lives.

Each of God's names in the Bible represents a way He wants us to trust Him. Do you trust Him to be your *Strength* (Psalm 18:1)? Is He your *Peace* (Ephesians 2:14)? Is He the *Lifter of Your Head* when you are down (Psalm 3:3)? Is He your *Refiner* (Malachi 3:2-3)? Your *Wisdom* (1 Corinthians 1:24)? Your *Counselor* (Psalm 16:7)? Your *Resting Place* (Jeremiah 50:6)? Each of His names is sacred, and we must treat each one as such.

When I worked in the secular entertainment world in Los Angeles, I heard the word "Jesus" a hundred times a day, spoken as a curse word by people with no reverence, love, or understanding of Him. It wasn't until I received Jesus that I realized exactly how much of a curse word that name was when it was used profanely. Taking God's name in vain brings a curse on whoever uses it in that manner because it breaks one of the Ten Commandments. "You shall not take the name of the LORD your God in vain, for the LORD will not hold him guiltless who takes His name in vain" (Exodus 20:7). It also violates God's *greatest* commandment, which is "you shall love the LORD your God with all your heart, with all your soul, with all your mind, and with all your strength" (Mark 12:30). No one who loves God uses His name in vain.

However, this same word—"Jesus"—when spoken in love by one who reverences Him, has great power in it. Power to save, deliver, heal, provide, protect, and so much more. Using it profanely shuts off these very things from our lives. There is also great power in each one of God's names, and when spoken with faith, love, understanding, and reverence, it brings a blessing and increases your faith.

For example, God's name is always a safe place to run to any time you need help. "The name of the LORD is a strong tower; the righteous run to it and are safe" (Proverbs 18:10). If you are sick, run to your Healer. If you can't pay your bills, run to your Provider. If you are afraid, run to your Hiding Place. If you are going through a dark time, run to your Everlasting Light. By speaking His name with reverence and thanksgiving, you invite Him to be that to you. Often there is so much we don't have in our lives simply because we do not acknowledge God as the answer to that need. How can you be healed if you don't acknowledge God as the Healer?

In the following list of God's names, I have included only 30. But there are hundreds more in His Word. Though

He is one God, there are so many dimensions to Him that in order for us to comprehend them all, He has given Himself many names. It's the only way we, who are so *small*, can begin to understand Him, who is so *great*. I suggest that every time you come across another name for God in the Bible, underline it or jot it in the margin or add it to a list. It will remind you of who God wants to be to you. As you read the following list, invite God to be each one of these names to you in a new, real, and life-changing way.

Thirty Good Names to Call Your God

1. *Healer* (Psalm 103:3)
2. *Redeemer* (Isaiah 59:20)
3. *Deliverer* (Psalm 70:5)
4. My *Strength* (Psalm 43:2)
5. *Shelter* (Joel 3:16)
6. *Friend* (John 15:15)
7. *Advocate* (1 John 2:1)
8. *Restorer* (Psalm 23:3)
9. *Everlasting Father* (Isaiah 9:6)
10. *Love* (1 John 4:16)
11. *Mediator* (1 Timothy 2:5-6)
12. *Stronghold* (Nahum 1:7)
13. *Bread of Life* (John 6:35)
14. *Hiding Place* (Psalm 32:7)
15. *Everlasting Light* (Isaiah 60:20)
16. *Strong Tower* (Proverbs 18:10)
17. *Resting Place* (Jeremiah 50:6)
18. *Spirit of Truth* (John 16:13)
19. *Refuge from the Storm* (Isaiah 25:4)
20. *Eternal Life* (1 John 5:20)
21. *The Lord Who Provides* (Genesis 22:14)
22. *Lord of Peace* (2 Thessalonians 3:16)
23. *Living Water* (John 4:10)
24. My *Shield* (Psalm 144:2)
25. *Husband* (Isaiah 54:5)
26. *Helper* (Hebrews 13:6)
27. *Wonderful Counselor* (Isaiah 9:6)
28. *The Lord Who Heals* (Exodus 15:26)
29. *Hope* (Psalm 71:5)
30. *God of Comfort* (Romans 15:5)

If you will go through this list of names periodically and speak each of them out loud, thanking God for being that to you, you'll be amazed at how your faith will grow and how much closer to God you will feel.

My Prayer to God

Lord, I draw close to You today, grateful that You will draw close to me as You have promised in Your Word (James 4:8). I long to dwell in Your presence, and my desire is for a deeper and more intimate relationship with You. I want to know You in every way You can be known. Teach me what I need to learn in order to know You better. I don't want to be a person who is "always learning and never able to come to the knowledge of the truth" (2 Timothy 3:7). I want to know the truth about who You are, because I know that You are near to all who call upon You in truth (Psalm 145:18).

I am open to whatever You want to do in me. I don't want to limit You by neglecting to acknowledge You in every way possible. I declare this day that You are my Healer, my Deliverer, my Redeemer, and my Comforter. Today I especially need to know You as (put in a name of the Lord). I believe You will be that to me.

God, help me to set aside time each day to meet with You alone. Enable me to resist and eliminate all that would keep me from it. Teach me to pray the way You want me to. Help me to learn more about You. Lord, you have said, "If anyone thirsts, let him come to Me and drink" (John 7:37). I thirst for more of You because I am in a dry place without You. I come to You this day and drink deeply of Your Spirit.

I know You are everywhere, but I also know that there are deeper manifestations of Your presence that I long to experience. Draw me close so that I may dwell in Your presence like never before.

God's Promises to Me

Draw near to God and He will draw near to you.
James 4:8

I will pray the Father, and He will give you another Helper, that He may abide with you forever—the Spirit of truth, whom the world cannot receive, because it neither sees Him nor knows Him; but you know Him, for He dwells with you and will be in you.
John 14:16-17

It is your Father's good pleasure to give you the kingdom.
Luke 12:32

Until now you have asked nothing in My name. Ask, and you will receive, that your joy may be full.
John 16:24

Let us hold fast the confession of our hope without wavering, for He who promised is faithful.
Hebrews 10:23

CHAPTER TWO

Lord, Cleanse Me and Make My Heart Right Before You

Before we go any further, let's get something straight. That is, you and I are not perfect. No one is perfect. None of us has arrived. None of us is incapable of sin. None of us is without problems. None of us have walked so long with the Lord that we know it all and therefore have nothing to learn. None of us is so complete that we don't need anything from God. None of us has it all together.

There! It's out in the open.

Please don't think I said this because I believe *you* need to know it. To the contrary, I believe you already *do* know it. I said it because I want you to know that we *all* know it. We know it about ourselves and we know it about each other. Therefore, we can be completely honest with ourselves about ourselves.

I don't want you to feel when reading this book that you have to live up to some impossibly high standard for your life. This book is not about living up to a standard. It's about letting *God* become your standard. It's not about trying to make something happen for yourself. It's recognizing that you *can't* make anything happen, but you *can* surrender your life to God and let *Him* make things happen. It's not about finding ways to avoid God's judgment and feeling like a failure if you don't do everything perfectly. It's about fully experiencing God's love and letting it perfect you. It's not about being somebody you are not. It's about becoming who you really are. But in order to see these things happen, you have to be completely honest with yourself and with God about who you are at the moment.

Women all over the world want to live fruitful lives. They want to dwell in God's grace while still obeying His laws. They want to be *unshakable* in God's truth yet *moved* by the suffering and needs of others. They want to know God in all the ways He can be known, and they want to be transformed by the power of His Spirit. But they are often hard on themselves when they don't see all these things happening on a daily basis. They are quick to observe all they are doing wrong and slow to appreciate all they are doing right.

For that reason, I want you to look upon this idea of cleansing your heart not as a judgment that your heart is dirty, but as God's call for you to get completely right before Him so He can bring all the blessings He has for you into your life. See it as God preparing you for the important work He has ahead for you to do.

In order to accomplish this, you have to examine your life closely. You have to be brave enough to say, "Lord, show me what is in my heart, soul, mind, spirit, and life that shouldn't be there. Teach me what I am not understanding. Convict me where I am missing the mark. Tear down my arrogance, pride, fear, and insecurities, and help me to see the truth about myself, my life, and my circumstances. Expose me to myself, Lord. I can take it. Enable me to correct the error of my ways. Help me to replace lies with truth and make changes that last."

It takes courage to pray a prayer like that. Perhaps more courage than many of us have at the moment. If you are hesitant to let the Lord expose your heart because of what He might reveal, then ask Him to give you the courage you need. In order to see positive changes happen in your life, you have to be open to the cleansing and stretching work of the Holy Spirit. You have to allow Him to expose your heart so you won't be deceived about yourself and your life. You have to invite Him to create a clean heart within you. Then be willing to do these two things:

1. *Confess* to God any sins of thought or action that He shows you.
2. *Repent* of the things you have just confessed.

True Confession

Don't think just because you are not a serial killer or have never robbed a bank that you don't have any sin to confess. Don't think because you have walked with the Lord for a number of years and go to church every Sunday morning and Wednesday night, and to all prayer meetings in between, that you have nothing for which you need to repent. Sin doesn't have to be glaring and obvious in order for it to be sin. For example, have you ever doubted that God can do what He promises in His Word? Doubt is a sin. Have you ever said anything about a person to someone else that isn't exactly flattering? Gossip is a sin. Have you ever avoided someone because you thought they might ask something of you that you didn't want to give? Selfishness is a sin. Have you ever had an unloving attitude toward another person? Whatever does not come from love is a sin.

Sin is hard to avoid 100 percent of the time. That's why confession is crucial. When we don't confess our sins, faults, or errors, they separate us from God. And we don't get our prayers answered. "Your iniquities have separated you from your God; and your sins have hidden His face from you, so that He will not hear" (Isaiah 59:2).

When we don't confess our sins, we end up trying to hide ourselves from God. Just like Adam and Eve in the garden, we feel we can't face Him. But the problem with attempting to hide from God is that it's impossible. The Bible says that everything we do will be made known. Even the things we said and thought in secret. "There is nothing covered that will not be revealed, nor hidden that will not be known. Therefore whatever you have spoken in the dark will be heard in the light, and what you have spoken in the ear in inner rooms will be proclaimed on the housetops" (Luke 12:2-3). "There is no creature hidden from His sight, but all things are naked and open to the eyes of Him to whom we must give account" (Hebrews 4:13).

What a frightening thought! If each of us will have to give an account, the quicker we get it straight with God the better. In fact, the sooner we deal with the sins we *can* see, the sooner God can reveal to us the ones we *can't*. And God only knows how much of that there is residing in each of us.

There is always a consequence for sin. King David described it best when he wrote of his own unconfessed sin: "When I kept silent, my bones grew old through my groaning all the day long. For day and night Your hand was heavy upon me; my vitality was turned into the drought of summer" (Psalm 32:3-4).

I remember having resentment toward my husband for words he said that hurt me deeply. As long as I held on to the hurt and resentment, it made me feel physically ill. I didn't want to confess it because I thought my feelings were justified and *he* was the one who was wrong. But I finally realized that all sin is sin, so I confessed my resentment to God as sin—and the moment I did, the feeling of sickness in my body left. "There is no soundness in my flesh because of Your anger, nor any health in my bones because of my sin. For my iniquities have gone over my head; like a heavy burden they are too heavy for me. My wounds are foul and festering because of my foolishness" (Psalm 38:3-5). Life is hard enough without us having to carry around old, dry, sick, weak bones.

Nothing is heavier than sin. We don't realize how heavy it is until the day we feel its crushing weight bringing death to our souls. We don't see how destructive it is until we smash into the wall that has gone up between us and God because of it. That's why it's best to confess every sin as soon as we are aware of it and get our hearts cleansed and right immediately. Confession gets sin out in the open before God. When you confess your sin, you're not informing God of something He doesn't know. He already knows. He wants to know that *you* know.

Confessing, however, is more than just apologizing. Anyone can do that. We all know people who are good apologizers. The reason they are so good at it is because they get so much practice. They have to say "I'm sorry" over and over again because they never change their ways. In fact, they sometimes say, "I'm sorry" without ever actually admitting to any fault. Those are the professional apologizers. And their confessions don't mean anything. But *true* confession means admitting in full detail what you have done and then fully *repenting* of it.

Full Repentance

It's one thing to recognize when you have done something that has violated God's laws; it's another to be saddened by it to such a degree that you are determined to never do it again. That's repentance. Repentance means to change your mind. To turn and walk the other way. Repentance means being so deeply sorry for what you have done that you will do whatever it takes to keep it from happening again. Confession means we *recognize* we have done wrong and *admit* our sin. Repentance means we are *sorry* about our sin to the point of grief, and we have *turned* and *walked away* from it.

Repenting of something doesn't necessarily mean we will never commit that sin again. It means we don't *intend* to ever commit it again. So if you find that you have to confess the same sin again after you have only recently confessed and repented of it, then do it. Don't let the enemy saddle you with guilt and ride on your back shouting words of failure in your ear. Confess and repent as many times as necessary to throw him off and see yourself win the battle over this problem. Don't entertain thoughts such as, *Surely God won't forgive me again for the same thing I just confessed to Him last week*. He forgives *every time* you confess sin before Him and fully repent of it. "Blessed is he whose transgression is forgiven, whose sin is covered" (Psalm 32:1). You can turn things around in your life when you turn to the Lord and repent.

Learn to confess and repent quickly so that the death process that is set in motion each time we violate God's rules is not given time to do it's full damage, "for the wages of sin is death" (Romans 6:23). Ask God every day to show you where your heart is not clean and right before Him. Don't let anything separate you from all God has for you.

My Prayer to God

Lord, I come humbly before You and ask You to cleanse my heart of every fault and renew a right spirit within me. Forgive me for thoughts I have had, words I have spoken, and things that I have done that are not glorifying to You or are in direct contradiction to Your commands. Specifically, I confess to You (name any thoughts, words, or actions that you know are not pleasing to God). I confess it as sin and I repent of it. I choose to walk away from this pattern of thought or action and live Your way. I know that You are "gracious and merciful, slow to anger and of great kindness" (Joel 2:13). Forgive me for ever taking that for granted.

Lord, I realize that You are a God who "knows the secrets of the heart" (Psalm 44:21). Reveal those to me if I am not seeing them. Show me any place in my life where I harbor sin in my thoughts, words, or actions that I have not recognized. Show me the truth about myself so that I can see it clearly. Examine my soul and expose my motives to reveal what I need to understand. I am willing to give up meaningless and unfruitful habits that are not Your best for my life. Enable me to make changes where I need to do so. Open my eyes to what I need to see so that I can confess all sin and repent of it. I want to cleanse my hands and purify my heart as You have commanded in Your Word (James 4:8).

I pray that You will "have mercy upon me, O God, according to Your lovingkindness; according to the multitude of Your tender mercies, blot out my transgressions. Wash me thoroughly from my iniquity, and cleanse me from my sin" (Psalm 51:1-2). Lord, "create in me a clean heart...and renew a steadfast spirit within me. Do not cast me away from Your presence, and do not take Your Holy Spirit from me" (Psalm 51:10-11). "Cleanse me from secret faults" (Psalm 19:12). "See if there is any wicked way in me, and lead me in the way everlasting" (Psalm 139:24). Make me clean and right before You. I want to receive Your forgiveness so that times of refreshing may come from Your presence (Acts 3:19).

God's Promises to Me

If we confess our sins, He is faithful and just to
forgive us our sins and to cleanse us from
all unrighteousness.
1 John 1:9

Beloved, if our heart does not condemn us, we have
confidence toward God. And whatever we ask we
receive from Him, because we keep His
commandments and do those things that
are pleasing in His sight.
1 John 3:21-22

I acknowledged my sin to You, and my iniquity I
have not hidden. I said, "I will confess my
transgressions to the Lord," and You forgave the
iniquity of my sin.
Psalm 32:5

Repent therefore and be converted, that your sins may be blotted out, so that times of refreshing may come from the presence of the Lord.
ACTS 3:19

He who covers his sins will not prosper, but whoever confesses and forsakes them will have mercy.
PROVERBS 28:13

Chapter Three

Lord, Help Me to Be a Forgiving Person

My mother was abusive when I was growing up, but my father wasn't. When I became a Christian, forgiving my mother was the obvious thing to do. It wasn't until years later that God revealed my unforgiveness toward my dad. When a Christian counselor I was speaking with about the unrest and frustration in my soul asked me if I had any unforgiveness toward my dad, I said no. Why would I? *He* wasn't the abusive parent. But when the counselor told me to pray and ask God to show me the truth, a lifetime of rage, anger, hurt, unforgiveness, and tears flooded my entire being. Down deep I felt my dad never came to my rescue. He never rescued me from my mother's insanity. He never came and let me out of the closet she had locked me in for so much of my early childhood. I didn't realize how much I blamed him for allowing my mother, who he knew was severely mentally ill, to treat me with such cruelty and abuse. When I forgave him that day, I felt peace like I had never known before.

Often we don't recognize the unforgiveness that is in us. We *think* we are forgiving, but we really aren't. If we don't ask God to reveal our unforgiveness to us, we may never get free of the paralyzing grip it has on our lives. A big part of making sure our lives are clean and right before God has to do with forgiving other people. We can never move into all God has for us unless we do.

An Excellent Choice

I know "hate" is a very strong word, and we hate to use the word "hate" about anything. And we certainly hate the thought that we might actually have hate for another person. But that's what unforgiveness is—the root of hate. When we entertain unforgiving thoughts, they turn to hate inside of us. Jesus felt so strongly about this that He said, "Whoever hates his brother is a murderer, and you know that no murderer has eternal life abiding in him" (1 John 3:15). He also said, "Whenever you stand praying, if you have anything against anyone, forgive him, that your Father in heaven may also forgive you your trespasses" (Mark 11:25).

Now let's get this straight. When we don't forgive, we are considered murderers without any eternal hope who shouldn't expect God to forgive us until we have forgiven others. I'd say that if it's between *forgiving* and *not forgiving*, forgiving seems like the better choice.

When we choose not to forgive, we end up walking in the dark (1 John 2:9-11). Because we can't see clearly, we stumble around in confusion. This throws our judgment off and we make mistakes. We become weak, sick, and bitter. Other people notice all this because unforgiveness shows in the face, words, and actions of those who have it. They see it, even if they can't specifically identify what it is, and they don't feel comfortable around it. When we choose to forgive, not only do *we* benefit, but so do the people around us.

Family First

It's very easy to have unforgiveness toward family members because they are with us the most, know us the best, and can hurt us the deepest. But for those very same reasons, unforgiveness toward one of them will bring the greatest devastation to our lives. That's why forgiveness must start at home.

First of all, it is very important to make sure you have forgiven your parents. The Bible is crystal clear about this issue. The fifth of the Ten Commandments says, "Honor your father and your mother, that your days may be long upon the land which the LORD your God is giving you" (Exodus 20:12). If you don't honor them it will shorten your life. And you can't fully honor them if you haven't forgiven them.

When I made the decision to forgive my mother, I did it because I wanted to obey God and move into all He had for me. It must have worked because look how old I am. But forgiving her once did not mean that I never had to worry about it again. There were layers and layers of unforgiveness that had built up in me over the years, and I found I had to forgive her every time one of them surfaced. Actually, I had to forgive her every time I saw her because she only became worse as the years went on.

Just because we confess our unforgiveness toward someone one day doesn't mean we won't have unforgiveness in us the next. That's why forgiveness is a choice we must make *every* day. We *choose* to forgive whether we feel like it or not. It's a decision, not a feeling. If we wait for good feelings, we could end up waiting a lifetime. If we have any bitterness or unforgiveness, it's always our fault for not choosing to let it go. It's our responsibility to confess it to God and ask Him to help us forgive and move on with our lives.

We also need to ask God to show us if we have any other family members we need to forgive. We don't tend to think of ourselves as unforgiving people. Irritated maybe, but not unforgiving. But we have to remember that our standards are much lower than God's, and therefore we often don't see where we need to forgive. Ask God to reveal any unforgiveness you have toward a family member. You are going to be miserable until you get it resolved.

When You Can't Forgive

Forgiveness is never easy. But sometimes it feels downright impossible in light of the devastating and horrendous pain we have suffered. If you have a hard time forgiving someone, ask God to help you. That's what I did regarding my mother, and by the time she died, I had absolutely no hard feelings toward her. If you can think of someone whom you find it hard to forgive, ask God to give you a heart of forgiveness for them. Pray for them in all the ways you can think of to pray. It's amazing how God softens our hearts when we pray for people. Our anger, resentment, and hurt turn into love.

Don't worry, however. When we forgive someone, it doesn't make them right or justify what they have done. It releases them into God's hands so *He* can deal with them. Forgiveness is actually the best revenge because it not only sets us free from the person we forgive, but it frees us to move into all God has for us. Our forgiving someone doesn't depend on them admitting guilt or apologizing. If it did, most of us would never be able to do it. We can forgive no matter what the other person does.

Sometimes incidents happen in our lives that are so devastating we can go for years without realizing the depth of the bitterness we have because of it. Sometimes we don't forgive *ourselves* for things we've done, and so we give ourselves a lifetime of punishment for whatever we did or did not do. Sometimes we blame God for things that have happened. Ask God to show you if any of these things are true about you. Don't let unforgiveness limit what God wants to do in your life.

Whatever It Takes

Four hundred and ninety times! That's how many times we have to forgive a person. Peter asked Jesus, "Lord, how often shall my brother sin against me, and I forgive him? Up to seven times?" Jesus said to him, "I do not say to you, up to seven times, but up to seventy times seven" (Matthew 18:21-22). You may be able to think of someone you have to forgive 490 times a *day*, but the point is that God wants you to forgive as many times as it takes. He wants you to be a forgiving person.

Jesus told the story of a man who was released from a large debt by his master. But he turned right around and made his own poor servant go to prison for not paying *him* a small debt. When the master heard about this he said, "I forgave you all that debt because you begged me. Should you not also have had compassion on your fellow servant, just as I had pity on you?" The master was so angry that he delivered that man to the torturers until he paid all that was due to him. Jesus said, "So My heavenly Father also will do to you if each of you, from his heart, does not forgive his brother his trespasses" (Matthew 18:32-35).

This is very serious. We who have received Jesus have been forgiven a *large* debt. We have no right to be unforgiving of others. God says, "Be kind to one another, tenderhearted, forgiving one another, just as God in Christ forgave you" (Ephesians 4:32). If we don't forgive, we will be imprisoned by our hatred and tortured by our bitterness.

Everything we do in life that has eternal value hinges on two things: loving God and loving others. It's far easier to love God than it is to love others, but God sees them as being the same. One of the most loving things we can do is forgive. It's hard to forgive those who have hurt, offended, or mistreated us. But God wants us to love even our enemies. And in the process of doing so, He perfects us (Matthew 5:48). It's always going to be easy to find things to be unforgiving about. We have to stop looking.

God wants you to move into all He has for you. But if you don't forgive, you get stuck where you are and shut off God's work in your life. Forgiveness opens your heart and mind and allows the Holy Spirit to work freely in you. It releases you to love God more and feel His love in greater measure. Life is worth nothing without that.

My Prayer to God

Lord, help me to be a forgiving person. Show me where I am not. Expose the recesses of my soul so I won't be locked up by unforgiveness and jeopardize my future. If I have any anger, bitterness, resentment, or unforgiveness that I am not recognizing, reveal it to me and I will confess it to You as sin. Specifically, I ask You to help me fully forgive (name anyone you feel you need to forgive). Make me to understand the depth of Your forgiveness toward me so that I won't hold back forgiveness from others. I realize that my forgiving someone doesn't make them right; it makes me free. I also realize that You are the only one who knows the whole story, and You will see justice done.

Help me to forgive myself for the times I have failed. And if I have blamed You for things that have happened in my life, show me so I can confess it before You. Enable me to love my enemies as You have commanded in Your Word. Teach me to bless those who curse me and persecute me (Matthew 5:44-45). Remind me to pray for those who hurt or offend me so that my heart will be soft toward them. I don't want to become hard and bitter because of unforgiveness. Make me a person who is quick to forgive.

Lord, show me if I have any unforgiveness toward my mother or father for anything they did or did not do. I don't want to shorten my life by not honoring them and breaking this great commandment. And where there is distance between me and any other family member because of unforgiveness, I pray You would break down that wall. Help me to forgive every time I need to do so. Where I can be an instrument of reconciliation between other family members who have broken or strained relationships, enable me to do that.

I don't want anything to come between You and me, Lord, and I don't want my prayers to be hindered because I have entertained sin in my heart. I choose this day to forgive everyone and everything, and walk free from the death that unforgiveness brings. If any person has unforgiveness toward me, I pray You would soften their heart to forgive me and show me what I can do to help resolve this issue between us. I know that I cannot be a light to others as long as I am walking in the darkness of unforgiveness. I choose to walk in the light as You are in the light and be cleansed from all sin (1 John 1:7).

God's Promises to Me

Judge not, and you shall not be judged. Condemn not, and you shall not be condemned. Forgive, and you will be forgiven.

Luke 6:37

The discretion of a man makes him slow to anger, and his glory is to overlook a transgression.

Proverbs 19:11

Love your enemies, bless those who curse you, do good to those who hate you, and pray for those who spitefully use you and persecute you, that you may be sons of your Father in heaven.

Matthew 5:44-45

He who hates his brother is in darkness and walks in darkness, and does not know where he is going, because the darkness has blinded his eyes.

1 John 2:11

If you forgive men their trespasses, your heavenly Father will also forgive you. But if you do not forgive men their trespasses, neither will your Father forgive your trespasses.

Matthew 6:14-15

CHAPTER FOUR

Lord, Teach Me to Walk in Obedience to Your Ways

I remember when I was in high school and had to take a required swimming class one semester. I hated it because it was at 7:30 every morning and my hair was ruined for the rest of the day. (There weren't any portable hair dryers back then, if you can even imagine such primitive times.) We had to swim daily, rain or shine, and it could get quite cold on those foggy California winter mornings. The only way I could be excused from swimming was if I were dying, and even then I had to have a note from the doctor.

In spite of the misery of that experience, I loved swimming and I became fairly good at it. I learned that if I was positioned correctly and did all the right moves, I could go forward quickly in the water. It became a smooth maneuver that would get me speedily to the other side of the giant pool. And nothing would make me falter—not even turbulence from other swimmers on either side of me.

The same principle is true for us. If we want to successfully navigate the waters of our lives, we must position ourselves correctly and learn all the right moves. If we don't, when we come to turbulent situations we will not be able to navigate through them. We will end up flailing around and exhausting ourselves just trying to stay afloat. And we will never actually get anywhere.

But when we position ourselves under the headship of Christ and learn to do what He requires of us, there is a flow of the Holy Spirit that will carry us wherever we need to go.

All the Right Moves

The way we learn what God expects of us is by reading His Word. We can't begin to make the right moves if we don't know what they are. And we can study all we want in this holy manual of life and learn everything we are supposed to do, but at some point we still have to jump in the water. The proof of our sincerity is in the *doing*, not just the knowing. It's one thing to make a list of do's and don'ts, but it's quite another to have a heart for God's ways and a soul that longs to live them out. It's one thing to read about life, it's another to live it. Obedience is something you *do*; having a heart to obey is something you *pray* about.

God, Help Me Be Disciplined

I hear this plea from women all over the world. We know a lot about what we're *supposed* to be doing, but we often have a hard time *doing* it. We must pray that God will enable us to be disciplined enough to do what we need to do.

I am a fairly disciplined person for the most part. But I wasn't always that way. There was a time in my life when I was the exact opposite. I was plagued with depression. And, as many of you who have been depressed know, you can't think clearly or organize your life well when you are struggling to find a reason to live. You are unable to do the things that are good for you because you don't know if you're worth it. You don't move forward in your life because it takes all your energy just to survive each day.

When I started learning to pray about every aspect of my life, I asked God to help me be disciplined enough to be daily in His Word, to pray faithfully, and to take the steps of obedience I needed to take. I asked Him to deliver me from depression and anything else that kept me from all He had for me. I was surprised at how quickly God answered those prayers. I have become disciplined, organized, and obedient beyond what I believe are my natural capabilities. I am still learning new levels of obedience, however, even after 32 years of walking with God. My body is getting older, but as a result of obeying God in new ways, my spirit is being renewed with each passing year. And with each new step of obedience I take, I experience new blessings and new freedoms I have not known before and never thought possible.

Don't fall into the trap of thinking that once you are saved you don't have to put forth any effort. That's like getting married and never taking a shower again. You might be able to get away with it for a while, but it's risky business and your quality of life will definitely suffer. Learning obedience is a lifelong process. There are always new dimensions of it to conquer. Even if you have walked with the Lord for 40 years, you still need to ask God to show you any area where you are not being obedient. *We get into trouble when we think we* know *what to do and we stop asking God if we're* doing *it.* "We must give the more earnest heed to the things we have heard, lest we drift away" (Hebrews 2:1).

We can never get prideful about how perfectly we are obeying God because He is continually stretching us and asking us to move into new levels of growth. Nor can we go to the other extreme, saying, "This is just the kind of person

I am—undisciplined and unteachable." We have no excuse for not doing what we need to do when God says He will *enable* us to do it if we will just call upon Him for help. All we have to say is, "Lord, help me to be disciplined enough to obey You the way You want me to so I can become the person You created me to be." Without the perfecting, balancing, refining work of His Holy Spirit, the freedom you have in Christ will turn into a license to do anything you want.

Personal Obedience

In addition to the rules we all have to obey, there are specific things God asks each of us to do as individuals in order to move us into the purpose He has for our lives. These are different for each person. For example, eight years ago God instructed my husband and me to move from California to Tennessee. This was not something I wanted to do nor did the thought of doing that ever enter my mind. I was happy where I was and didn't want to leave. But because it was a clear directive from God, we packed up and obeyed. The reasons why we moved have become increasingly evident over the years, and I am so grateful we heard God's directive and followed it. But we probably wouldn't have heard if we hadn't actually said the words, "Lord, show us what we are supposed to be doing."

It's important that you keep asking God to show you what He wants *you* to do. If you don't ask, you won't know. It's that simple. For example, God may ask you to take a different job, stop a certain activity, join a certain church, or change the way you've always done something. Whatever He asks you to do, remember He does this for your greatest blessing. But you must understand that you may not hear Him speaking to you at all if you are not taking the other steps of obedience He expects all of us to take that are found in His word. "One who turns away his ear from hearing the law, even his prayer is an abomination" (Proverbs 28:9). It doesn't hurt to ask.

Doing Things You'd Rather Not

We all have to do things we don't want to do. In even the most wonderful of jobs, there are still aspects of it that we don't enjoy. But part of being successful in life means doing things we would rather not. When we do things we don't like simply because we know we need to do them, it builds character in us. It makes us disciplined. It forms us into a leader God can trust. And there is always a price to pay when we forsake the things we *need* to do in order to do only the things we *feel* like doing. We must be willing to make sacrifices for the blessings we want.

When you find it difficult to do what you *know* you need to, ask the Holy Spirit to help you. Of course, you still have to take the first step, no matter how daunting, intimidating, dreadful, uncomfortable, or distasteful. But when you do, the Holy Spirit will assist you the rest of the way. "I will put My Spirit within you and cause you to walk in My statutes, and you will keep My judgments and do them" (Ezekiel 36:27).

Ten Good Reasons to Obey God

There are countless reasons to obey God, but there is one primary reason: He said to. If there were no other reason, that would certainly be enough. However, there are many important benefits that you and I should be reminded of regularly, and below I've listed ten good ones.

1. *We get our prayers heard.* "If I regard iniquity in my heart, the Lord will not hear. But certainly God has heard

me; He has attended to the voice of my prayer" (Psalm 66:18-19).

2. *We enjoy a deeper sense of the Lord's presence.* "If anyone loves Me, he will keep My word; and My Father will love him, and We will come to him and make Our home with him" (John 14:23).

3. *We gain wisdom.* "He stores up sound wisdom for the upright; He is a shield to those who walk uprightly" (Proverbs 2:7).

4. *We have God's friendship.* "You are my friends if you do whatever I command you" (John 15:14).

5. *We can live safely.* "You shall observe My statutes and keep My judgments, and perform them; and you will dwell in the land in safety" (Leviticus 25:18).

6. *We are perfected.* "Whoever keeps His word, truly the love of God is perfected in Him. By this we know that we are in Him" (1 John 2:5).

7. *We are blessed.* "Behold, I set before you today a blessing and a curse: the blessing, if you obey the commandments of the LORD your God which I command you today" (Deuteronomy 11:26-27).

8. *We find happiness.* "Happy is he who keeps the law" (Proverbs 29:18).

9. *We have peace.* "Mark the blameless man, and observe the upright; for the future of that man is peace" (Psalm 37:36).

10. *We have a long life.* "My son, do not forget my law, but let your heart keep my commands; for length of days and long life and peace they will add to you" (Proverbs 3:1-2).

A Stepping-Stone to Destiny

God has great plans for you. He has important things He wants you to do. And He is preparing you for your destiny right now. But you have to take steps of obedience in order to get there. And you have to trust that He knows the way and won't hurt you in the process.

God's rules are for our benefit, not to make us miserable. When we live by them, life works. When we don't, life falls apart. When we obey, we have clarity. When we don't, we have confusion. And there is a definite connection between obedience and the love of God. Even though God loves us, we won't sense His love if we are walking in disobedience to His ways.

There is also a direct connection between obedience and getting your prayers answered (1 John 3:22). If you have been frustrated because you don't see answers to your prayers, ask God if it is because of disobedience. Say, "Lord, is there any area of my life where I am not obeying You?" Don't keep telling God what *you* want without asking Him what *He* wants.

You never know when you will step into the moment for which God has been preparing you. And it is not just one moment; it's many successive ones. It doesn't matter whether you are a single career woman or a married lady with nine children under the age of ten, it doesn't matter whether you are nineteen or ninety, God is preparing you daily for something great. He wants you to be willing to let Him purify you, fortify you, and grow you up in Him. But you have to play by the rules. "If anyone competes in athletics, he is not crowned unless he competes according to the rules" (2 Timothy 2:5). You can't swim into the mainstream of those moments successfully if you are not doing all the right moves now.

My Prayer to God

Lord, Your Word says that those of us who love Your law will have great peace and nothing will cause us to stumble (Psalm 119:165). I love Your law because I know it is good and it is there for my benefit. Enable me to live in obedience to each part of it so that I will not stumble and fall. Help me to obey You so that I can dwell in the confidence and peace of knowing I am living Your way.

My heart wants to obey You in *all* things, Lord. Show me where I am not doing that. If there are steps of obedience I need to take that I don't understand, I pray You would open my eyes to see the truth and help me to take those steps. I know I can't do all things right without Your help, so I ask that You would enable me to live in obedience to Your ways. "With my whole heart I have sought You; oh, let me not wander from Your commandments!" (Psalm 119:10).

Your Word says that "if we say we have no sin, we deceive ourselves, and the truth is not in us" (1 John 1:8). I don't want to deceive myself by not asking You where I am missing the mark You have set for my life. Reveal to me when I am *not* doing things I *should* be doing. Show me if I'm doing things I should not. Help me to hear Your specific instructions to me. Speak to me clearly through Your Word so I will know what's right and what's wrong. I don't want to grieve the Holy Spirit in anything I do (Ephesians 4:30). Help me to be ever learning about Your ways so I can live in the fullness of Your presence and move into all You have for me.

GOD'S PROMISES TO ME

Whatever we ask we receive from Him, because we keep His commandments and do those things that are pleasing in His sight.

1 JOHN 3:22

For the LORD God is a sun and shield; the LORD will give grace and glory; no good thing will He withhold from those who walk uprightly.

PSALM 84:11

He who keeps His commandments abides in Him, and He in him. And by this we know that He abides in us, by the Spirit whom He has given us.

1 JOHN 3:24

Blessed are those who hear the word of God and keep it!

LUKE 11:28

He who has My commandments and keeps them, it is he who loves Me. And he who loves Me will be loved by My Father, and I will love him and manifest Myself to him.

JOHN 14:21

CHAPTER FIVE

Lord, Strengthen Me to Stand Against the Enemy

When an unthinkable tragedy burst upon our nation on September 11 in New York City, many people asked, "Why did this happen?" In their unbearable grief and shock they wanted an answer. There are many answers to that question, but the main one is this: We have an enemy. I don't mean just we the people of New York or we the people of the United States. I mean we the people who stand for the things of God. There is an enemy who opposes all that God is and everything He does and anyone who believes in Him or tries to live His way.

We all have an enemy who is like a terrorist to our soul. If we don't realize this, it will be easy for him to manipulate us. Of course, he is not omniscient nor omnipresent—he can't be everywhere and know our every thought—but if we don't fully realize that he is a limited and defeated foe, then we will be harassed by him continually. One of the things Jesus accomplished when He died and rose again was to break the power of the enemy. When He defeated the enemy on the cross, He gave us authority over him. He said,

"I give you the authority…over all the power of the enemy, and nothing shall by any means hurt you" (Luke 10:19).

We are all involved in a spiritual battle with an enemy who will never let up. Even though it is people who do evil things to us, we have to keep in mind that it is our ultimate enemy, the devil, who is behind it. "For we do not wrestle against flesh and blood, but against principalities, against powers, against the rulers of the darkness of this age, against spiritual hosts of wickedness in the heavenly places" (Ephesians 6:12). Even when we are being attacked by a person, recognizing who our real enemy is will be the first step in standing strong against him.

Just as God has a plan for you, so does Satan. Satan's plan is to steal from you and destroy your life. "The thief does not come except to steal, and to kill, and to destroy" (John 10:10). He disguises himself so that he doesn't look threatening, and he lulls you into thinking that you are not in any danger (2 Corinthians 11:14). But he never takes a day off. He is constantly trying to see his plan for your life fulfilled. That's why you have to "be sober, be vigilant; because your adversary the devil walks about like a roaring lion, seeking whom he may devour" (1 Peter 5:8).

For the most part, we are able to recognize obvious attacks of the enemy. But the more subtle ones, when we are being seduced into accepting something into our lives that will ultimately get us offtrack or destroy us, are harder to recognize. For example, he will attempt to make you believe you deserve every bad thing that happens to you. But deserving is not the issue with God. We didn't deserve to have Jesus die for us. Yet He did. The point is not whether we deserve the things the devil throws our way. The point is Jesus died so we don't have to experience them. Ask God to help you discern the enemy's work in your life. Then "resist the devil and he will flee from you" (James 4:7).

Five Good Weapons Against Mass Destruction

God has given us many weapons to use against the enemy's plan for our destruction. Here are the top five:

1. *A powerful weapon against the enemy is God's Word.* This is *the most* powerful weapon. Jesus Himself used it against the devil when He was led into the wilderness by the Holy Spirit and Satan came to tempt Him (Matthew 4:1). One would think that if you were the Son of God you wouldn't have to go into the wilderness at all, let alone to be tempted by the devil. But "the tempter came to Him" the way he comes to all of us, and Jesus used the Word of God to refute him. He said, "Man shall not live by bread alone, but by every word that proceeds from the mouth of God" (Matthew 4:4). When the devil tries to destroy your life, refute him with God's Word. "A prudent man foresees evil and hides himself; the simple pass on and are punished" (Proverbs 27:12). The moment you identify evil working in your midst, hide yourself in the Word of God.

2. *A powerful weapon against the enemy is praise.* The devil hates it every time we worship God. That's because he can't tolerate people worshiping anyone else but him. He detests it so much he can't even be around it. When we praise and worship God, His presence dwells powerfully in our midst and the devil has to leave.

3. *A powerful weapon against the enemy is obedience.* If we are living in sin or walking in disobedience in any way, this leaves the door open in our lives for the devil to gain a point of entry and ultimately a foothold. Bad things happen to us that might be the enemy's work, but it could also be because our own sin has given him a place to erect a stronghold in

our life. Satan does not have jurisdiction over you, but disobedience to the laws of God opens the door and puts out a welcome mat for him. Confession and repentance will shut the door in his face.

4. *A powerful weapon against the enemy is faith*. Keep in mind that the enemy is always planting land mines out ahead of you. You have no idea where they are because they are not visible to the human eye. The way to avoid them is to walk closely with God and let Him guide your steps. That takes faith. "Resist him, steadfast in the faith, knowing that the same sufferings are experienced by your brotherhood in the world" (1 Peter 5:8-9). Walking in faith is a powerful way to avoid the enemy's trap.

5. *A powerful weapon against the enemy is prayer and fasting*. Prayer is a strong weapon against the enemy. Fasting makes it even more so. Often the hold of the enemy upon our lives can only be broken by prayer and fasting. It doesn't seem as though such a simple thing could do so much, but it does. And it might not seem as though anything is happening while you fast, but there are powerful things being broken in the spirit realm. Often just a simple 24-hour fast is enough to break the hold of the enemy upon our lives. Regular fasts will keep evil at bay and strongholds broken down. It's a way of saying, "I deny myself what I want most and put God first in my life." The enemy hates that because he knows it's a sure way of resisting and defeating him.

I'm a Good Person, so Why Is He Attacking Me?

Many people have asked this question, but the question answers itself. The enemy attacks you *because* you are a good person. The devil will always attack anyone who loves God and lives His way. In fact, this is the main criteria for his enmity against you. The only way you could get him to not do that is to become like him. You would have to stand for what he represents. As long as you have a heart for the things of God, you are his target.

Keep in mind that the greater your commitment is to the Lord, the more the devil will try to harass you. That's why if you are moving into a deeper level of commitment to God, or coming into a new time of deliverance and freedom, or entering into new ministry or work God is opening up for you, you can depend on your enemy trying to stop it. He will do all he can to wear you down with discouragement, sickness, confusion, guilt, strife, fear, depression, or defeat. He may try to threaten your mind, your emotions, your health, your work, your family, or your relationships. He will try to get you to give up. Even though he is not close to being as powerful as God, he attempts to make you think otherwise. He will try to gain a point of rule in your life through deception. He will try to blind you to the truth and get you to believe his lies. He will try to convince you he is winning the battle, but the truth is that he has already lost.

This is the deal. The devil has come to steal, kill, and destroy. Jesus has come to give you life abundantly. Hmm. Let's see. Death and destruction from Satan. Life and abundance from Jesus. Does that mean if you're not living a life of abundance then the devil must be robbing you? I think that's a good possibility, especially since this is his life goal. The only other possibility is that you have not truly aligned yourself with God and are not living His way. Ask God to show you the truth about your situation. Don't let the enemy of your soul talk you into accepting anything less than what God has for you.

My Prayer to God

Lord, I thank You for suffering and dying on the cross for me, and for rising again to defeat death and hell. My enemy is defeated because of what You have done. Thank You that You have given me all authority over him (Luke 10:19). By the power of Your Holy Spirit I can successfully resist the devil and he must flee from me (James 4:7). Show me when I am not recognizing the encroachment of the enemy in my life. Teach me to use that authority You have given me to see him defeated in every area.

Reveal to me any place in my life where I am walking in disobedience. If I have given the enemy a place in my protective armor through which he can secure a hook, show me so I can rectify it. Gird me with strong faith in You and in Your Word. Help me to fast and pray regularly in order to break any stronghold the enemy is trying to erect in my life.

Lord, I know that in the midst of the battle I don't have to be fainthearted. I don't have to be afraid in the face of the enemy (Deuteronomy 20:3). Thank You that even though the enemy tries to take me captive to do his will, You have given me the power to escape his snares completely (2 Timothy 2:26). Thank You that You have delivered me from him (Psalm 18:17) and You are my shield because I live Your way (Proverbs 2:7). Help me to "not be overcome by evil," but instead give me the strength to "overcome evil with good" (Romans 12:21). Hide me in the secret place of Your presence from the plots of evil men (Psalm 31:20). Thank You that I will never be brought down by the enemy as long as I stand strong in You.

GOD'S PROMISES TO ME

The Lord is faithful, who will establish you and guard you from the evil one.

2 THESSALONIANS 3:3

Take up the whole armor of God, that you may be able to withstand in the evil day, and having done all, to stand. Stand therefore, having girded your waist with truth, having put on the breastplate of righteousness, and having shod your feet with the preparation of the gospel of peace; above all, taking the shield of faith with which you will be able to quench all the fiery darts of the wicked one. And take the helmet of salvation, and the sword of the Spirit, which is the word of God; praying always with all prayer and supplication in the Spirit, being watchful to this end with all perseverance and supplication for all the saints.

EPHESIANS 6:13-18

When the whirlwind passes by, the wicked is no more, but the righteous has an everlasting foundation.

PROVERBS 10:25

Be strong in the Lord and in the power of His might. Put on the whole armor of God, that you may be able to stand against the wiles of the devil.

EPHESIANS 6:10-11

Chapter Six

Lord, Show Me How to Take Control of My Mind

I remember one particular Friday afternoon when my husband was out of town on a trip and my children were each spending the night at a friend's house. With everyone away it was a rare opportunity for me to have some quiet time and get a lot of writing done.

Much to my surprise, however, I felt tremendous loneliness and sadness after they left. I thought about everything that was wrong with my life, and it made me hopelessly depressed. It was so bad I couldn't think about anything else. These thoughts paralyzed me to such a degree that I wasn't able to call anyone, go anywhere, catch up on mail, or do any work around the house. And, of course, I didn't get any writing done. I just sat crying in my room with the Bible open on my lap.

"Lord, show me what's the matter with me and what I should do about it," I prayed. "I am going to fast until I hear from You or this thing breaks."

I fasted through Saturday and into the night. About 4:00 Sunday morning I awoke with deep anxiety in my soul. I got up and began reading my Bible. When my eyes fell upon the words in Isaiah about exchanging "the garment of praise for the spirit of heaviness" (Isaiah 61:3), I knew in that instant I was dealing with a spirit of heaviness. There was nothing wrong with me or my life, but the enemy was trying to get me to believe there was.

For the next 20 minutes I sang praises to God and spoke His Word out loud. I told the enemy to get away from me, and I thanked the Lord for giving me the authority to do that. Then, as clearly as I have ever felt anything, I sensed the dark, heavy blanket of spiritual oppression lift. It lifted so suddenly and completely that I realized I had been dealing with a direct and specific attack from the enemy.

As I look back, I believe it was because I was in the middle of writing *The Power of a Praying® Wife* and the enemy was trying to make me give up. But the opposite happened. In the days ahead I had new vision for my life and my future, and a renewed commitment to identifying and resisting the enemy's lies. I realized I should have caught his lies the minute they entered my mind instead of entertaining them as truth.

Take Control

A big part of standing against the enemy of our souls is taking control over our minds. As the Bible says, we must learn to bring every thought into captivity (2 Corinthians 10:5).

It was an astounding revelation to me as a new believer when I learned that I didn't have to entertain every thought that came into my head. I had a choice about whether to listen to them or not. Many serial killers talk about how they heard a voice in their head telling them to kill and they just followed orders. When people are not raised to discern the voices in their head, they don't recognize the voice of the devil. He is a clever deceiver who will come to each one of us and try to speak lies into our minds. We have to be ready for him.

The Lies We Believe

Do you ever have certain thoughts that play over and over in your mind like an old broken record? Have you ever had a thought come to your mind that produces a physical feeling in your body, such as a pain in your heart, a queasy sensation in the pit of your stomach, tightness in your throat, weakness in your arms and legs, tears in your eyes, a rash on your face and neck? Do "what if" thoughts ever plague your mind, such as "What if I jumped off the balcony?" or "What if I ran my car into that wall?" Have you ever had "if only" thoughts? Such as, "If only I hadn't done that." "If only I had been there." "If only I would have said something." Do you ever have self-punishing thoughts? "No one cares about me." "I'm such a failure." "I'm no good." "Nothing I do turns out right."

If you've had thoughts like these, please know that this is not God giving you revelation for your life. It is the enemy trying to gain control of your mind.

Life has much suffering, but too often we suffer unnecessarily because of lies we believe about ourselves and our circumstances. We accept as fact the words that are spoken to our souls by an enemy who wants us destroyed. We can become fearful, depressed, lonely, angry, doubtful, confused, insecure, hopeless, beaten down, worried, and full of self-pity, all because of lies we believe. But we can overcome each one of these lies with prayer, faith, and the truth of God's Word.

You must be aware, however, that one of the enemy's tactics is to try and steal God's Word from you. He will do that by getting you to question God's Word, just as he did with Eve in the Garden. "Did God really say that?" "Does God really mean that?" "Will God really mind if you do that?" "Does God really care about you?"

Then he will contradict God's Word. "God didn't say that." "God doesn't mind that." "God doesn't think you're worth much." "God's withholding good things from you."

When the thoughts that you think begin to question and contradict God's Word, you are being set up by your enemy. Remember, "there is a way that seems right to a man, but its end is the way of death" (Proverbs 14:12). Certain thoughts may appear to you to be accurate, but when you hold them up next to God's Word, the lie is exposed.

Deception is the enemy's ongoing plan of attack. Jesus said the devil "was a murderer from the beginning, and does not stand in the truth, because there is no truth in him. When he speaks a lie, he speaks from his own resources, for he is a liar and the father of it" (John 8:44). The *only* power the devil has is in getting people to believe his lies. If they don't believe his lies, he is powerless to get his work done.

Choose Your Thoughts Carefully

You have a choice about what you will accept into your mind and what you won't. You can choose to take every thought captive and "let this mind be in you which was also in Christ Jesus" (Philippians 2:5), or you can allow the devil to feed you lies and manipulate your life. Every sin begins as a thought in the mind. "For from within, out of the heart of men, proceed evil thoughts, adulteries, fornications, murders, thefts, covetousness, wickedness, deceit, lewdness, an evil eye, blasphemy, pride, foolishness" (Mark 7:21-22). If you don't take control of your mind, the devil will.

That's why you must be diligent to monitor what you allow into your mind. What TV shows, magazines, and books do you look at? What music, radio programs, or CDs do you listen to? Do they fill your mind with godly thoughts and feed your spirit so you feel enriched, clear-minded, peaceful, and blessed or do they deplete you and leave you feeling empty, confused, anxious, and fearful? "God is not the author of confusion but of peace" (1 Corinthians 14:33). When we fill our minds with God's Word and godly books and magazines written by people in whom God's Spirit resides, and we listen to music that praises and glorifies Him, we leave no room for the enemy's propaganda.

If you want to determine whether your thoughts are from the enemy or the Lord, ask yourself, "Are these thoughts I would *choose* to have?" If you answer no, then they are probably from your enemy. If, for example, you are sitting in church and you suddenly envision the choir naked, recognize where this is coming from. Rather than beat yourself up for having impure thoughts, tell the enemy to get off your brain because you will not allow your soul to be a dumping ground for his trash. Tell him you "have the mind of Christ" and you won't listen to anything that is inconsistent with that (1 Corinthians 2:16).

Refusing to entertain unrighteousness in your thought life is part of resisting the devil. How many people have we known who should have done that and didn't?

You don't have to live with confusion or mental oppression. You don't have to "walk as the rest of the Gentiles walk, in the futility of their mind, having their understanding darkened, being alienated from the life of God, because of the ignorance that is in them, because of the hardnening of their heart" (Ephesians 4:17-18). Instead you can have clarity and knowledge. Even though your enemy tries to convince you that your future is as hopeless as his, or that you are a failure with no purpose, value, gifts, or abilities, God says exactly the opposite. Believe God and don't listen to anything else.

My Prayer to God

Lord, help me to never exchange Your truth for a lie. Where I have accepted a lie as truth, reveal that to me. Help me to clearly discern when it is the enemy who is speaking. I don't want to think futile and foolish thoughts or give place to thoughts that are not glorifying to You (Romans 1:21). I don't want to walk according to my own thinking (Isaiah 65:2). I want to bring every thought captive and control my mind.

Your Word is "a discerner of the thoughts and intents of the heart" (Hebrews 4:12). As I read Your Word, may it reveal any wrong thinking in me. May Your Word be so etched in my mind that I will be able to identify a lie of the enemy the minute I hear it. Spirit of Truth, keep me undeceived. I know You have given me authority "over all the power of the enemy" (Luke 10:19), and so I command the enemy to get away from my mind. I refuse to listen to lies.

Thank You, Lord, that I "have the mind of Christ" (1 Corinthians 2:16). I want Your thoughts to be my thoughts. Show me where I have filled my mind with anything that is ungodly. Help me to resist doing that and instead fill my mind with thoughts, words, music, and images that are glorifying to You. Help me to think upon what is true, noble, just, pure, lovely, of good report, virtuous, and praiseworthy (Philippians 4:8). I lay claim to the "sound mind" that You have given me (2 Timothy 1:7).

GOD'S PROMISES TO ME

Do not be conformed to this world, but be transformed by the renewing of your mind, that you may prove what is that good and acceptable and perfect will of God.

ROMANS 12:2

Though we walk in the flesh, we do not war according to the flesh. For the weapons of our warfare are not carnal but mighty in God for pulling down strongholds, casting down arguments and every high thing that exalts itself against the knowledge of God, bringing every thought into captivity to the obedience of Christ.

2 CORINTHIANS 10:3-5

To be carnally minded is death, but to be spiritually minded is life and peace.

ROMANS 8:6

Put off, concerning your former conduct, the old man which grows corrupt according to the deceitful lusts, and be renewed in the spirit of your mind, and...put on the new man which was created according to God, in true righteousness and holiness.

EPHESIANS 4:22-24

You will keep him in perfect peace, whose mind is stayed on You, because he trusts in You.

ISAIAH 26:3

Chapter Seven

Lord, Rule Me in Every Area of My Life

I know a young man who has a heart for God and is tremendously gifted to lead worship and teach the Word. But he can't bring himself to fully surrender his life to the Lord. He continues to live his own way, doing his own thing, and is constantly frustrated that nothing has worked out in his life—not only his personal life, but also his career and finances. I know if he would just say, "Whatever You want, Lord, I will do it" and truly live that out, God would use him powerfully and every part of his life would be blessed.

Why do some people never seem to grow in the Lord? Why is it they go from one calamity to the next, never able to get beyond survival mode? Why do they seldom, if ever, experience the joy of the Lord? Spritual breakthrough? A deeper of relationship with Him? The release to step out in the area of their gifting? Why can't they move forward into the purposes and destiny God has for them?

The answer, I believe, lies in the word "surrender." They have not fully surrendered everything to God. They have not truly made Jesus Lord over their lives.

Surrendering everything means being willing to say, "Lord, whatever You want me to do I'll do it. I say yes to anything You ask of me, even it means dying to myself and my desires. I will give up the things of the flesh that I want in order to have more of You in my life. I will go to church when I feel like staying home. I will fast when I feel like eating. I will pray when I would rather go to bed. I will read Your Word when I would rather watch TV. I will give when I would rather spend my money on myself. I will enter into praise and worship as my first reaction instead of my last resort. I will do whatever You say so that I can please You and move into all You have for me." This attitude of surrender means putting God first and submitting to His rulership. And it makes all the difference in our lives.

Jesus is Lord whether we declare it or not. That's because "God also has highly exalted Him and given Him the name which is above every name, that at the name of Jesus every knee should bow, of those in heaven, and of those on earth, and of those under the earth, and that every tongue should confess that Jesus Christ is Lord, to the glory of God the Father" (Philippians 2:9-11). But He is not only Lord over the universe, He is Lord over our individual lives as well. Whether we acknowledge that or not will determine the success and quality of our life. If we don't personally declare Jesus to be Lord over our lives, it shows we are not controlled by the Spirit. "No one can say that Jesus is Lord except by the Holy Spirit" (1 Corinthians 12:3). It reveals we are still controlled by the flesh.

Whatever You Say, Lord

Do you remember watching old western movies where the good guy (in the white shirt) catches the bad guy (in the black shirt) and points his gun at him and says, "Stick 'em up!" (It just doesn't sound as menacing to say, "Stick *them* up.")

The bad guy drops everything, raises his hands, and says, "I give up."

Well, this is the kind of surrender God wants. Only you are not the bad guy and God is not pointing a gun at you. He is pointing His finger. But not in an accusatory or embarrassing way. He is pointing to you in a loving way, just as He would if He had picked you for His team. He is saying, "You! I want you! Surrender to Me so I can give you all that I have for you."

If we would drop everything and say, "I give up, Lord. I surrender. Take everything. I will do whatever You say," our lives would be better in every way.

Why is it so hard for us to simply say, "Whatever You want, Lord. I'll do anything You ask"? It's because we want what we want and we're afraid of what God might ask of us. We think He might do something to hurt us. Also, it's not just a matter of *saying*, "Jesus is Lord." We must then *do* what He *says*. Jesus said, "Why do you call Me 'Lord, Lord,' and do not do the things which I say?" (Luke 6:46). We doubt that what God asks us to do will be for our greatest blessing. But that's wrong. God just wants us to be on the winning team.

If you feel you aren't experiencing any breakthrough in your life, check to see if you have truly surrendered yourself to the Lord. Have you given Jesus that place of Lordship? Have you let go of everything? If not, lift your hands and take that first step.

Jesus said, "Whoever does not bear his cross and come after Me cannot be My disciple" (Luke 14:27). You can't bear His cross unless you surrender your life to Him. A surrendered life, a life ruled entirely by God, is one that can be used powerfully for His kingdom purposes. God doesn't want just part of you. He wants it all. Pray that you will give God what He wants.

My Prayer to God

Lord, I bow before You this day and declare that You are Lord over every area of my life. I surrender myself and my life to You and invite You to rule in every part of my mind, soul, body, and spirit. I love You with all my heart, with all my soul, and with all my mind. I commit to trusting You with my whole being. I declare You to be Lord over every area of my life today and every day.

Enable me to deny myself in order to take up my cross daily and follow you (Luke 9:23). I want to be Your disciple just as You have said in Your Word (Luke 14:27). Help me to do what it takes. I want to lose my life in You so I can save it (Luke 9:24). Teach me what that means. Speak to me so that I may understand.

Help me to say yes to You immediately when You give me direction for my life. My desire is to please You and hold nothing back. I surrender my relationships, my finances, my work, my recreation, my decisions, my time, my body, my mind, my soul, my desires, and my dreams. I put them all in Your hands so they can be used for Your glory. I declare this day that "I have been crucified with Christ; it is no longer I who live, but Christ lives in me; and the life which I now live in the flesh I live by faith in the Son of God, who loved me and gave Himself for me" (Galatians 2:20). Rule me in every area of my life, Lord, and lead me into all that You have for me.

GOD'S PROMISES TO ME

If anyone desires to come after Me, let him deny himself, and take up his cross daily, and follow Me. For whoever desires to save his life will lose it, but whoever loses his life for My sake will save it.
LUKE 9:23-24

If we live, we live to the Lord; and if we die, we die to the Lord. Therefore, whether we live or die, we are the Lord's.
ROMANS 14:8

As you have therefore received Christ Jesus the Lord, so walk in Him, rooted and built up in Him and established in the faith, as you have been taught, abounding in it with thanksgiving.
COLOSSIANS 2:6-7

Trust in the LORD with all your heart, and lean not on your own understanding; in all your ways acknowledge Him, and He shall direct your paths.
PROVERBS 3:5-6

Therefore humble yourselves under the mighty hand of God, that He may exalt you in due time, casting all your care upon Him, for He cares for you.
1 PETER 5:6-7

Chapter Eight

Lord, Take Me Deeper in Your Word

Some time ago I went into the hospital for emergency surgery. I stayed there about two weeks and then spent six weeks at home with a nurse. I had eight months of recovery after that. It was over a year before I was even close to being back to normal. (I'll give you more details about this in a later chapter.)

During that time in the hospital I was too sick and weak and in too much pain to read the Word. I was hooked up to a machine with tubes running in and out of my body, so I couldn't sit up or turn over. That meant holding a heavy Bible was out of the question. Because I needed round-the-clock care, my sister organized my husband, children, and close friends to spend specific times with me. Each person took a three-hour shift on different days, except for my daughter, who took a twelve-hour shift from 8:00 every night until 8:00 in the morning. This was extremely difficult for her because she was in college at the time and had to be up with me every couple hours at night and then go to school all day. Besides everything else these loving people did for me, I depended on them to read the Word of God to me.

When I was sent home with a nurse, I had to be isolated from all people except my immediate family members because of the risk of infection. During that time, no one was able to read the Bible to me because they were too busy. (I don't say that as a criticism; they each had to take care of me plus do the work I usually do in addition to their own full-time work.) It was a considerable strain for everyone.

So during that time I spent convalescing at home I listened to the Bible on tape. But it wasn't the same as reading it myself. I don't retain information as well when I hear it as I do when I read it. Also, on tape the speaker keeps talking without stopping. I found I would get caught up thinking about a verse I'd just heard and then not hear the next ten. Normally, when I read the Word myself, I go over each verse slowly and thoroughly, especially the ones speaking to me at that moment. I let it digest in my inner being, and I ask God to teach me new things that I haven't seen before.

Even after I began to recover and was able to sit up and read the Word myself, my mind was so foggy and my eyes so blurry from all the anesthetic and drugs I'd had to take every day that I had a hard time absorbing it. I knew the problem was in *me*, but the Bible wasn't speaking to me like it used to, and I felt helpless as to what to do about it. Reading the Word had always been life-giving for me, but now it became more of a duty. I read because I knew I needed to.

Another factor in all this was that I couldn't go to church for five months, so I wasn't being taught the Word from the pulpit or from a Bible study. I had not been without that type of teaching for longer than two weeks at a time since I had become a believer 31 years before. I listened to tapes of sermons, but my mind wandered, and I often fell asleep in the middle of them.

Because I didn't have regular feeding in the Word of God the way I usually had, I began to lose ground in my life. It became harder to make decisions because I didn't hear God's voice as clearly as I used to. It was difficult to write because I couldn't focus on what God wanted me to say. But most of all I felt empty inside. It wasn't until I thought to actually *pray* about the problem itself that I experienced breakthrough in this area. I prayed, "Lord, I need to have Your Word come alive to me again. Make that happen, Father. Clear my mind and soul. Teach me new things. Help me to go deeper into Your Word than ever before."

About a week after I started praying that prayer, God answered it. The Bible became fresh and exciting again. I found new revelation. New understanding. I decided if God answered that simple prayer, then why shouldn't we pray *every* time we read the Bible, "Lord, take me deeper into Your Word"? Our time in God's Word is one of the most important aspects of our lives, and it should be covered in prayer.

Daily Bread for Our Souls

God's Word is food for our souls. We can't live without it. It is written that "man shall not live by bread alone, but by every word that proceeds from the mouth of God" (Matthew 4:4). If we are not continually fed with God's Word, we will starve spiritually.

In those months when I was in the hospital and recovering, I was amazed at how much of the Word I lost from my memory. I realize that all the medicine and anesthetic I had in me contributed a lot to that, but I was shocked that I couldn't remember certain Scriptures I used to quote so easily. After all those years of reading the Bible, how could

I lose so much so quickly? Of course, there are some Scriptures that are engraved in my brain and soul that I probably could recite in my sleep, but I realized then how important it is for each of us to *guard* the Word of God that has been deposited in our souls. "Therefore we must give the more earnest heed to the things we have heard, lest we drift away" (Hebrews 2:1). We don't realize how quickly it can be stolen from us.

Be a Doer of the Word

It doesn't matter how long you walk with God; He always has new things for you to learn. It may be new dimensions of what you already know, or it may be something you have never seen before. Either way, it's not enough to just *learn* the truth; you must *act* on it. "Be doers of the word, and not hearers only, deceiving yourselves. For if anyone is a hearer of the word and not a doer, he is like a man observing his natural face in a mirror; for he observes himself, goes away, and immediately forgets what kind of man he was" (James 1:22-24). If we don't *do* what the Word says, we not only *forget* it but we also forget who we are in the process.

Whenever you read God's Word, it is essential to ask Him to help you practically apply it to your life. Take a step that indicates you believe what you read and are going to live like it. If you don't, what you know of the Word will be taken from you. It's possible to *hear* the Word, *read* the Word, and even *teach* the Word and still remain unchanged and unaffected. All Scripture will teach us, convict us, enrich us, heal us, warn us, and expose our hearts. But we have to act on it. That's why you have to ask God to speak to you every time you read His Word and show you what you should be doing in response to it.

Ten Good Reasons to Read God's Word

If you have trouble being in God's Word every day, here are just a few of the many reasons to read the Bible that should inspire you:

1. *To know where you are going.* You can't foresee the future or *exactly* where you are heading, but God's Word will guide you. "Direct my steps by Your word, and let no iniquity have dominion over me" (Psalm 119:133).

2. *To have wisdom.* Knowledge of God's Word is where wisdom begins to grow in you. "The law of the LORD is perfect, converting the soul; the testimony of the LORD is sure, making wise the simple" (Psalm 19:7).

3. *To find success.* When you live according to the teachings of the Bible, life works. "This Book of the Law shall not depart from your mouth, but you shall meditate in it day and night, that you may observe to do according to all that is written in it. For then you will make your way prosperous, and then you will have good success" (Joshua 1:8).

4. *To live in purity.* You must live a life of holiness and purity in order to enjoy more of the Lord's presence, but you can't be made pure without being cleansed through God's Word. "How can a young man cleanse his way? By taking heed according to Your word" (Psalm 119:9).

5. *To obey God.* If you don't understand what God's laws are, how can you obey them? "Teach me, O LORD, the way of Your statutes, and I shall keep it to the end. Give me understanding, and I shall keep Your law; indeed, I shall observe it with my whole heart. Make me walk in the path of Your commandments, for I delight in it" (Psalm 119:33-35).

6. *To have joy.* You cannot be free of anxiety and unrest without the Word of God in your heart. "The statutes of the LORD are right, rejoicing the heart; The commandment of the LORD is pure, enlightening the eyes" (Psalm 19:8).

7. *To grow in faith.* You can't grow in faith without reading and hearing the Word of God. "So then faith comes by hearing, and hearing by the word of God" (Romans 10:17).

8. *To find deliverance.* You won't know what you need to be free of unless you study God's Word to find out. "If you abide in My Word, you are My disciples indeed. And you shall know the truth, and the truth shall make you free" (John 8:31-32).

9. *To have peace.* God will give you a peace that the world can't give, but you must find it first in His Word. "Great peace have those who love Your law, and nothing causes them to stumble" (Psalm 119:165).

10. *To distinguish good from evil.* Everything has become so relative today, how can you know for sure what is right and wrong without God's Word? "Your Word I have hidden in my heart, that I might not sin against You!" (Psalm 119:11).

Going for the Gold

God has gold nuggets and diamonds everywhere in His Word, but we must dig them out. And, just like precious gems and metals when they are first pulled from the ground, the treasures of God's Word need to be polished and refined in us in order to have the brilliance they are capable of revealing. Every time you go over one of God's promises in your heart, it will become more refined and polished in you and shine more brightly in your soul.

One of the most priceless gems you will find in God's Word is His voice. That's because He speaks to us through His Word as we read it or hear it. In fact, we can't really learn to recognize God's voice to our soul if we are not hearing Him speak to us first in His Word. The more you hear it, the easier it is to recognize, and the less chance you will accept a counterfeit.

There were countless times in my early walk with the Lord when I was still suffering from depression and anxiety that I turned to his Word. All it took was reading the Bible for a few minutes, and I would feel calm and hopeful again. That's because the Word straightens out our mind and soul and helps us think clearly about things. It leads us away from self-destructive thoughts and enables us to enjoy a sense of well-being. It gives us hope and keeps us on course. It provides us a solid foundation upon which to build a life of wholeness. Ask God to meet you in His Word every day. He looks forward to that, and He wants you to also.

There is no way to draw closer to God, or have a clean and right heart before Him, or be a forgiving person, or walk in obedience to His ways, or take control of your mind, or stand against the enemy, or make Jesus Lord of your life unless you are in the Word of God every day. It's your compass. Your guide. You can't get where you need to go without it.

My Prayer to God

Lord, I thank You for Your Word. "Your Word is a lamp to my feet and a light to my path" (Psalm 119:105). It is food to my soul, and I can't live without it. Enable me to truly comprehend its deepest meaning. Give me greater understanding than I have ever had before, and reveal to me the hidden treasures buried there. I pray that I will have a heart that is teachable and open to what You want me to know. I desire Your instruction. Teach me so I may learn.

Help me to be diligent to put Your Word inside my soul faithfully every day. Show me where I'm wasting time that could be better spent reading Your Word. Give me the ability to memorize it. Etch it in my mind and heart. Make it become a part of me. Change me as I read it.

Lord, I don't want to be just a hearer of Your Word. Show me how to be a doer of Your Word as well. Enable me to respond the way I should and obey You. Show me when I am not doing what it says. Help me to apply my heart to Your instruction and my ears to Your Words of knowledge (Proverbs 23:12). May Your Word correct my attitude and remind me of what my purpose is on earth. May it cleanse my heart and give me hope that I can rise above my limitations. May it increase my faith and remind me of who You are and how much You love me. May it bring the security of knowing my life is in Your hands and You will supply all my needs.

Thank You, Lord, that when I look into Your Word I find You. Help me to know You better through it. Give me ears to recognize Your voice speaking to me every time I read it (Mark 4:23). I don't want to ever miss the way You are leading me. When I hear Your voice and follow You, my life is full. When I get off the path You have for me, my life is empty. Guide, perfect, and fill me with Your Word this day.

God's Promises to Me

The Word of God is living and powerful, and sharper than any two-edged sword, piercing even to the division of soul and spirit, and of joints and marrow, and is a discerner of the thoughts and intents of the heart.

Hebrews 4:12

He who looks into the perfect law of liberty and continues in it, and is not a forgetful hearer but a doer of the work, this one will be blessed in what he does.

JAMES 1:25

Blessed is the man who walks not in the counsel of the ungodly, nor stands in the path of sinners, nor sits in the seat of the scornful; but his delight is in the law of the LORD, and in His law he meditates day and night. He shall be like a tree planted by the rivers of water, that brings forth its fruit in its season, whose leaf also shall not wither; and whatever he does shall prosper.

PSALM 1:1-3

Whoever keeps His word, truly the love of God is perfected in him. By this we know that we are in Him.

1 JOHN 2:5

He who heeds the word wisely will find good, and whoever trusts in the LORD, happy is he.

PROVERBS 16:20

Chapter Nine

Lord, Instruct Me as I Put My Life in Right Order

Tabitha was a disciple of Christ. A *female* disciple! This means she was a believer who followed faithfully the teachings of Jesus. She also did many good works and charitable deeds which benefited others. As a result, she was dearly loved.

Some time after Jesus was crucified and had risen, Tabitha became ill and died. Several men went to find Peter, one of the original 12 disciples, and bring him back to where Tabitha's body was being prepared for burial. When Peter arrived at the house, he went to the upper room where she had been laid. He asked the women who were weeping over her to leave him alone in the room, and then he knelt down to pray.

When Peter finished praying, he turned toward the dead woman's body and said, "Tabitha, arise." Immediately she opened her eyes and sat up. Extending his hand to her, Peter helped her to her feet. When all the people saw that Tabitha had been brought back from the dead, many believed in the Lord (Acts 9:36-42).

There is nothing else known about Tabitha, but from this short account of her life it's clear that she was a woman who had her priorities in order. She loved the Lord. She loved others. She had a servant's heart. She lived her life in a way that pleased God and blessed people. All this information about her is found in that one word—"disciple."

When trouble came into Tabitha's life and she was struck down even to the point of death, God sent one of His faithful disciples to pray for her and raise her up again. Would this have happened if she were just a nominal believer, living on the distant edge of the life God wanted her to live? Would this have happened if she didn't love God? Didn't love others? Didn't have a servant's heart? Didn't give of herself? Didn't obey? I don't think so. Her life was in order and God blessed her because of it. And He gave her a second chance. That's what He wants to do for us if we will put Him first.

Top Priority

We can't live successfully without right priorities in our lives. Yet some of us try to do that every day. Correct priorities are not something we can figure out on our own. We have to be led by the Holy Spirit and have a clear knowledge of God's Word in order to understand what they should be.

Our two most important priorities come directly from the Word of God. Jesus told us about them saying, "'You shall love the LORD your God with all your heart, with all your soul, and with all your mind.' This is the first and great commandment. And the second is like it: 'You shall love your neighbor as yourself'" (Matthew 22:37-39). It can't get much clearer than that. If you maintain these two top priorities—love God and love others—they will guide you in setting all the other priorities in your life.

Your relationship with the Lord must always have top priority over everything else. The Lord said, "You shall have no other gods before Me" (Exodus 20:3), and He means it. God wants your *undivided* attention. When you seek Him first every day and ask Him to help you put your life in order, He will do that. I know from experience, and I'm sure you do too, that when we don't seek God first, our lives get out of control. As a result, our lives start ruling *us* instead of us being in charge of *them*.

God is a God of order. We can tell that by looking at the universe. None of it is random or accidental. He doesn't want our lives to be either. His will is that we "let all things be done decently and in order" (1 Corinthians 14:40). And when we pray to Him about it, He will help us do just that. He will show us how to align ourselves under proper authority so that we can come under the covering of His protection. This is crucial to our moving into all God has for us.

The Submission Issue

Submission is something you *decide* to do, not something someone *forces* you to do. The meaning of the word "submit" is "to submit yourself." It's a condition of the heart. Having a submitted heart means you are *willing* to submit yourself and come into proper alignment in accordance with God's will.

Our first priority in submission must always be to "submit to God" (James 4:7). This means you do not have to submit to the wishes of anyone who asks you to do something that is against God's commands. You can have a submitted heart and still be able to draw the line when what is being asked of you violates your conscience and the laws of God.

For example, if a person who is a designated authority over your life asks you to do something that is wrong, or if that person says or does something to you that is inappropriate and violates what is right in the sight of God, you must decline to be a party to it and declare it to be wrong. But you don't have to scream at the person saying, "You idiot! You fool! What is the matter with you? Get behind me, Satan!" Instead, give them a respectful explanation such as, "With all due respect, I believe that what you are asking me to do is a violation of the laws of God, and I could not with any good conscience do it, knowing it would bring God's judgment on us both." Or "What you just said and did to me is offensive in the eyes of God, and I must tell you that such inappropriate behavior will not serve either of us well."

The difference between having a submitted heart and one that is not is that one will garner blessings for you and the other will get you into trouble.

Jesus Himself was submitted to God. His priorities were definitely in order. God wants that "this mind be in you which was also in Christ Jesus, who, being in the form of God, did not consider it robbery to be equal with God, but made Himself of no reputation, taking the form of a bondservant, and coming in the likeness of men. And being found in appearance as a man, He humbled Himself and became obedient to the point of death, even the death of the cross" (Philippians 2:5-8). Now that's submission! It would seem that if anyone might not have to be in perfect submission it would be Jesus. Yet in order to accomplish God's purpose for His life, He was submitted to the will of the

Father, even to the point of unfathomable suffering and death. What a role model He is for all of us.

When Trust Is Violated

Many women have a problem with submission because their trust has been violated or they were hurt in the past when they submitted to someone. No one wants to be a doormat or the object of another person's abuse. God does not want that either. Nor is He asking you to be a mindless robot. That's why you must pray for wisdom about this issue. It is a highly sensitive one, and you need to discern what the Lord is telling you.

For those of you who have had a terrible experience with this issue, I want to encourage you. God is not asking you to be stupid, sacrifice your sanity for a principle, or suffer at the hand of an abuser. He will give you wisdom when you ask for it. If you find yourself going along with someone who violates the Word of God and His holy laws, not to mention your own conscience, that's not submission. That's just dumb. Don't let yourself go there.

I know of a woman who submitted to an abusive husband, and he ended up killing her. She wasn't spiritually discerning because she didn't put God first and seek Him as to what to do. She stayed in that violent relationship until it turned disastrous instead of doing what was necessary to find help. That is *not* submission, that's foolishness.

I know of another woman who refused to submit to her husband in any way, and she ended up losing her whole family and her home. Because she had been sexually violated by a leader in her church when she was a teenager, she would not consider trusting any man enough to submit to him.

There has to be a balance. And that balance can only be found by submitting to *God first*. Ask Him to help you discern exactly to whom you are to be submitted and in what way. Don't just submit blindly or ignorantly. Know what you are doing. When your heart's desire is to do what's right and be in right order, God will help you find that perfect balance.

It All Falls into Place

The Bible says we should submit to authority figures designated by God in our church, in our family, in our work, and in our government. To be in right order and have our lives work well, we need to be planted in a church home. It gives us a base of operation. We can't get as far as God wants us to go without it.

Each church has a unique distinction and purpose, and you will not be happy until you find the one God has for you. This doesn't mean you have to go to a different church every week until you find one that is perfect and makes you 100 percent happy. Those don't exist. Churches are, after all, made up of imperfect people like us. What it does mean is that you need to ask God to show you where your church family is.

When you are in the church you are supposed to be in, you will recognize the pastor's voice as an important spiritual authority in your life. Again, you need to have wisdom and the leading of the Lord. If the authority figures in your church get offtrack and there is immorality, financial corruption, unbiblical teaching, or sin, then you should not be subject to that kind of leadership. Ask God to lead you away from an unholy alignment.

We all need a pastor, a strong Christian leader, or a mentor speaking truth into our lives. God will help you discern who that is. Don't get me wrong, this is not a case for having a guru. The spiritual authority in your life is God's *messenger*, not someone to be worshiped instead of God. This is also not a gender issue. The Bible says, "there is neither male or female; for you are all one in Christ Jesus" (Galatians 3:28). This is about having someone in your life to speak truth to you in love and cover you in prayer.

Beyond your submission to God and your submission to other designated authorities in your life, you must be in right relationship to other people, "submitting to one another in the fear of God" (Ephesians 5:21). Submission to others takes a heart that loves others as ourselves. That's the key. When you love God first and others second, all the other priorities in your life will fall into place and you will be in right order. When you ask God to show you clearly what your priorities should be, He will.

My Prayer to God

Lord, I pray You would help me set my life in right order. I want to always put You first above all else in my life. Teach me how to love You with all my heart, mind, and soul. Show me when I am not doing that. I don't want to have any other gods but You in my life. Show me if I have lifted up my soul to an idol. My desire is to serve You and only You. Help me to live accordingly.

Give me a submissive heart. Help me to always submit to the governing authorities and the correct people in my family, work, and church. Show me who the proper spiritual authorities are to be in my life. Plant me in the church you want me to be in. Help me to move into proper alignment in every area of my life by willingly submitting myself to others where I need to do so. Show me clearly to whom I am to be submitted and how I am to do it. Give me discernment and wisdom about this. Show me any time I am not submitted to the right people in the right way.

I know that if my life is not in proper order I will not receive the blessings You have for me. But I also know that if I seek You first, all that I need will be added to me (Matthew 6:33). I seek You first this day and ask that You would enable me to put my life in perfect order. May I never come out from under the covering of spiritual protection You have placed in my life.

God's Promises to Me

Seek first the kingdom of God and His righteousness, and all these things shall be added to you.
Matthew 6:33

He who finds his life will lose it, and he who loses his life for My sake will find it.
Matthew 10:39

All of you be submissive to one another, and be clothed with humility, for "God resists the proud, but gives grace to the humble."
1 Peter 5:5

And this commandment we have from Him: that he who loves God must love his brother also.
1 John 4:21

Obey those who rule over you, and be submissive, for they watch out for your souls, as those who must give account. Let them do so with joy and not with grief, for that would be unprofitable for you.
Hebrews 13:17

CHAPTER TEN

Lord, Prepare Me to Be a True Worshiper

When I used to work as a singer, dancer, and actress on television during the time when musical variety shows were at their peak, I would have to sing a song over and over all day long while I was rehearsing it with the choreography. Then I had to sing it over and over again in the evening as we prerecorded it for the show the next day. It had to be prerecorded because when I was dancing and singing at the same time, I could not be miked for sound. There were no portable headsets back then as there are now. I used to go home at night after the last session of the day and could hardly sleep because the music and lyrics of the songs we had been working on would still be playing over and over in my mind. I could not get them out of my head.

That is exactly what happens to us when we hear and sing praise and worship songs over and over. They continue to play in our mind, soul, and spirit even when we are not actually worshiping God. Even when we are sleeping.

I learned that principle years ago when I became a believer. Back then when I suffered with severe depression, there were countless times I would get up in the middle of the night to sing or speak praises to the Lord in order to get rid of it. I had gone to several doctors about it, but the medicine they gave me only seemed to cover up the problem. It was always still there when the medicine wore off. I'm not saying that people shouldn't take medicine if they are depressed. I'm saying it didn't solve the problem for *me*. I had suffered from depression from the time I was a young child and was locked in a closet by my mother. The hopelessness, futility, and sadness I felt about myself and my life made it hard to get through each day. I needed an infusion of the joy of the Lord, and that's what praising God did for me.

When I praised and worshiped God, it was like being hooked up to a spiritual IV. As long as I had my heart and eyes lifted to God in worship and praise, the joy of the Lord poured into my body, mind, soul, and spirit and crowded out the darkness and depression. It worked every time.

I started buying praise and worship songs on tape and later CDs. I played them in the car as I drove, in the bathroom when I was drying my hair, in the kitchen as I was cooking, through the house when I was doing housework, or at my desk when I was writing letters or going through the mail. Sometimes I would sing along to them, but other times I would just let the music play through my mind and spirit. It amazed me that confusion, oppression, fear, or anxiety couldn't exist in the heart of a worshiping child of God. Eventually, I got free of depression completely.

Nothing we do is more powerful or more life-changing than praising God. It is one of the means by which God transforms us. Every time we praise and worship Him, His presence comes to dwell in us and changes our hearts and allows the Holy Spirit to soften and mold them into whatever He wants them to be.

Because praise and worship is not something our flesh naturally *wants* to do, we have to *will* ourselves to do it. And because it's not the first thing we think of to do, we have to decide to do it no matter what our circumstances. We have to say, "I *will* praise the Lord." Of course, the more we get to know God, the easier praise becomes. When we get to the point where we can't keep from praising Him, then we are at the place we are supposed to be. If you ever find yourself unmotivated in this regard, try reading the following 20 reasons to worship God from Psalm 103. It works for me every time.

Twenty Good Reasons to Worship God

1. *He forgives my iniquities.*
2. *He heals all my diseases.*
3. *He redeems my life from destruction.*
4. *He crowns me with lovingkindness.*
5. *He satisfies my mouth with good things.*
6. *He executes righteousness and justice for the oppressed.*
7. *He makes His ways known.*
8. *He is merciful.*
9. *He is gracious.*
10. *He is slow to anger.*
11. *He will not strive with us.*
12. *He will not keep His anger forever.*
13. *He does not punish us according to our iniquities.*
14. *He shows great mercy to those who fear Him.*
15. *He removes our transgressions from us.*
16. *He has pity on us.*
17. *He remembers we are dust.*
18. *His mercy is everlasting.*
19. *He blesses our children and grandchildren who obey Him.*
20. *He rules over all and His throne is established.*

Worship His Way

We can claim to know and love God, but if we are not worshiping and praising Him every day, we are in the dark about who He really is. "Although they knew God, they did not glorify Him as God, nor were thankful, but became futile in their thoughts, and their foolish hearts were darkened" (Romans 1:21). We shut off so much in our lives when we don't give God the glory due Him. We don't want to be wandering around in the dark entertaining futility in our minds, all because we are not *true* worshipers of our awesome God.

Five God Ways to Praise the Lord

God wants us to give our whole self to worshiping Him, and He wants us to do it *His* way.

1. *God wants us to sing our praises to Him.* "Praise the LORD! For it is good to sing praises to our God; for it is pleasant, and praise is beautiful" (Psalm 147:1). "Serve the LORD with gladness; come before His presence with singing" (Psalm 100:2).

2. *God wants us to lift our hands to Him.* "Lift up your hands in the sanctuary, and bless the LORD" (Psalm 134:2).

3. *God wants us to speak our praise to Him.* "Therefore by Him let us continually offer the sacrifice of praise to God, that is, the fruit of our lips, giving thanks to His name" (Hebrews 13:15).

4. *God wants us to praise Him with dancing and instruments.* "Let them praise His name with the dance; let them sing praises to Him with the timbrel and harp" (Psalm 149:3).

5. *God wants us to praise Him together with other believers.* "I will declare Your name to My brethren; in the midst of the assembly I will sing praise to You" (Hebrews 2:12).

Praising and worshiping God with other believers is one of the most powerful and significant things we can do in our lives. Corporate worship causes bondages to be broken, and it makes the way for wonderful changes in us that might never happen otherwise. A powerful dynamic occurs in the spirit realm when we worship God together that can't happen any other way.

No matter what your church background is or has been, ask God to make you into the true worshiper He wants you to be. Give your whole self to it. As long as you have breath you can "rejoice always, pray without ceasing, in everything give thanks; for this is the will of God in Christ Jesus for you" (1 Thessalonians 5:16-18). The songs of worship you sing over and over in your heart in the day will fill your soul in the night.

My Prayer to God

Lord, there is no source of greater joy for me than worshiping You. I come into Your presence with thanksgiving and bow before You this day. I exalt Your name for You are great and worthy to be praised. Thank You that "You have put gladness in my heart" (Psalm 4:7). All honor and majesty, strength and glory, holiness and righteousness are Yours, O Lord.

Thank You that You are "gracious and full of compassion, slow to anger and great in mercy" (Psalm 145:8). Thank You that You are "mighty in power" and Your "understanding is infinite" (Psalm 147:5). Thank You that You lift up the humble and cast the wicked down (Psalm 147:6). Thank You that You execute justice for the oppressed, You give food to the hungry, and You give freedom to the prisoners. Thank You that You open the eyes of the blind and raise up those who are bowed down (Psalm 146:7-8).

Thank You, Lord, that Your plans for my life are good, and You have a future for me that is full of hope. Thank You that You are always restoring my life to greater wholeness. I praise You and thank You that You are my Healer, my Deliverer, my Provider, my Redeemer, my Father, and my Comforter. Thank You for revealing Yourself to me through Your Word, through Your Son, Jesus, and through Your mighty works upon the earth and in my life. Thank You for Your love, peace, joy, faithfulness, grace, mercy, kindness, truth, and healing. Thank You that I can depend on You, for You and Your Word are unfailing. Thank You that You are the same yesterday, today, and tomorrow.

Lord, forgive me when I neglect to praise and worship You as You deserve and desire. Teach me to worship You with my whole heart the way You want me to. Make me a *true* worshiper, Lord. May praise and worship of You be my first response to every circumstance.

I praise Your name this day, Lord, for You are good and Your mercy endures forever (Psalm 136:1). "Because Your lovingkindness is better than life, my lips shall praise You. Thus I will bless You while I live; I will lift up my hands in Your name" (Psalm 63:3-4). I will declare Your "glory among the nations" and Your "wonders among all peoples" (Psalm 96:3). I worship You in the splendor of Your holiness and give You the glory due Your name (Psalm 29:2).

GOD'S PROMISES TO ME

But the hour is coming, and now is, when the true worshipers will worship the Father in spirit and truth; for the Father is seeking such to worship Him. God is Spirit, and those who worship Him must worship in spirit and truth.

JOHN 4:23-24

Offer to God thanksgiving, and pay your vows to the Most High. Call upon Me in the day of trouble; I will deliver you, and you shall glorify Me.

PSALM 50:14-15

Let all those rejoice who put their trust in You; let them ever shout for joy, because You defend them; let those also who love Your name be joyful in You. For You, O LORD, will bless the righteous; with favor You will surround him as with a shield.

PSALM 5:11-12

Whoever offers praise glorifies Me; and to him who orders his conduct aright I will show the salvation of God.

PSALM 50:23

I will praise You with my whole heart; before the gods I will sing praises to You. I will worship toward Your holy temple, and praise Your name for Your lovingkindness and Your truth; for You have magnified Your word above all Your name. In the day when I cried out, You answered me, and made me bold with strength in my soul.

PSALM 138:1-3

Chapter Eleven

Lord, Bless Me in the Work I Do

I know what it's like to go to bed hungry. When I was a child, we were so poor there were many times when we had no food in the house and no way of getting any. That feeling of hunger was frightening, and the fear never left me, even after I grew up. In fact, this fear caused me to always work hard in order to ensure it would never happen again. It drove me to take every baby-sitting job I could get, for 50 cents an hour on weekends, instead of being with my friends when I was a young teenager. It's what made me work after school most days and into the night, plus all day Saturday and Sunday, when I was in high school and college. Even after I left college and was in the workforce, I held down *two* jobs instead of one for the same reason. Always in the back of my mind was the fear that there wouldn't be enough money for food, so I often labored beyond what my body and mind could take.

It wasn't until I came to know the Lord and began to understand the way He provides for His children that I finally got rid of the fear. It was such a relief to discover that I could trust *God* to take care of me. I no longer had to kill myself in desperation; I could look to Him for everything I needed.

I also became more discerning about the work I was doing. I no longer had to take any and every job I could get. Instead, I asked God what work *He* wanted me to do. I found that when I was led by the Lord in the work I did, and I committed all my work to Him for His glory, He blessed it. It was no longer drudgery. I prayed God would help me do it well, and as a result, my work soon became fruitful, successful, and fulfilling.

Everyone Has a Job to Do

It doesn't matter if you are a stay-at-home mom, a full-time student, a CEO of a giant corporation, a single woman who is self-supporting, a married woman running a home, a skilled career woman, a disabled person, a baby-sitter, a house sitter, a single working mom, or a volunteer at the rescue mission downtown—you have work to do. It doesn't matter if your work is recognized by the whole world or only God sees it. It doesn't matter if you are getting paid big bucks or receiving no financial compensation whatsoever. Your work is valuable. And you want it to be blessed by God.

Whatever work we do, we want to do it well and be successful. When our work is good, it gives us fulfillment. When we accomplish something worthwhile that makes life better for other people, our families, or ourselves, it gives us satisfaction. But when the work of our hands is not blessed, we are weighed down with frustration and unfulfillment.

The ideal woman described in the Bible is a hard worker (Proverbs 31). She buys and sells property (a real estate agent?). She plants a vineyard (a landscaper?). She makes clothing (a designer?). And she sells it (manager of a clothing store?). She is a woman of strength, energy, and vision who works hard into the night and knows that what she has to offer is good. God wants us to experience that kind of success and satisfaction. But it doesn't happen without prayer.

Prayer helps us to find the balance between being "greedy for gain," which depletes our life (Proverbs 1:19), and having "a slack hand," which makes us poor (Proverbs 10:4). Prayer helps us to not "overwork to be rich" (Proverbs 23:4-5) yet still be diligent in our work, which may ultimately bring us monetary rewards (Proverbs 10:4). Prayer helps us find the balance between laziness and obsession, between gaining the whole world and losing our own soul (Matthew 16:26).

The Bible says that "the laborer is worthy of his wages" (1 Timothy 5:18). This means you deserve to be paid or rewarded for your work. Sometimes the reward is in the actual doing of it itself. You don't get paid for maintaining a home, serving soup at the rescue mission, or teaching a child to tie his shoes, but your reward for seeing the result of your labor is priceless. "The labor of the righteous leads to life" (Proverbs 10:16).

If you have a paying job, don't hesitate to pray that you will be compensated fairly and generously. Pray for your employer to be blessed in his business so he in turn can afford to pay all employees well. Pray that your work is recognized and appreciated by others. Pray to receive promotions and advancement in line with God's will. Say, "Lord, I would like to have that promotion and that raise if it's Your will for my life." As you pray that way and commit your work to the Lord, He will bless it.

No matter what your paycheck reflects, your work is important to God, it's important to others, and it's important to you. You can't afford not to pray about it. Commit your work to the Lord and ask Him to bless it.

My Prayer to God

Lord, I pray You would show me what work I am supposed to be doing. If it is something other than what I am doing now, reveal it to me. If it is something I am to do in addition to what I am already doing, show me that too. Whatever it is You have called me to do, both now and in the future, I pray You will give me the strength and energy to get it done well. Enable me to do what I do successfully. May I find great fulfillment and satisfaction in every aspect of it, even the most difficult and unpleasant parts.

Thank You that in all labor there is profit of one kind or another (Proverbs 14:23). I pray that the rewards of my work will be great. May I always be compensated fairly and richly out of the storehouse of Your abundance. Bless the people I work for and with. May I always be a blessing and a help to each one of them. As I come in contact with others in my work, I pray that Your love and peace will flow through me and speak loudly of Your goodness. Enable me to touch them for Your kingdom.

Lord, I thank You for the abilities You have given me. Where I am lacking in skill help me to grow and improve so that I do my work well. Teach me to excel so that the result of what I do will be pleasing to others. Open doors of opportunity to use my skills and close doors that I am not to go through. Give me wisdom and direction about that.

I commit my work to You, Lord, knowing You will establish it (Proverbs 16:3). May it always be that I love the work I do and be able to do the work I love. According to Your Word I pray that I will not lag in diligence in my work, but remain fervent in spirit, serving You in everything I do (Romans 12:11). Establish the work of my hands so that what I do will find favor with others and be a blessing for many. May it always be glorifying to You.

God's Promises to Me

Blessed is every one who fears the LORD, who walks in His ways. When you eat the labor of your hands, you shall be happy, and it shall be well with you.

PSALM 128:1-2

The blessing of the LORD makes one rich, and He adds no sorrow with it.

PROVERBS 10:22

Let the beauty of the LORD our God be upon us, and establish the work of our hands for us; yes, establish the work of our hands.

PSALM 90:17

Do you see a man who excels in his work? He will stand before kings; he will not stand before unknown men.

PROVERBS 22:29

Every man should eat and drink and enjoy the good of all his labor; it is the gift of God.

ECCLESIASTES 3:13

CHAPTER TWELVE

Lord, Plant Me so I Will Bear the Fruit of Your Spirit

My dad was a farmer for most of his life. He knew how to plant and grow healthy crops. The main thing I learned from him was how to grow a garden of vegetables and fruit. We didn't have the fancy tools people have today—just a shovel and a hoe. We didn't even have running water or indoor plumbing, let alone a sprinkler system outside. We had to wait for the irrigation water to come through our land and then channel it to where the crops were by digging little furrows for the water to travel on either side of the rows of seed. That way it would water the roots without washing the seedlings or young plants away.

After we planted the seeds and watered them, we nurtured, fed, and tended the soil around the seeds so they could grow without hindrance. We also tried to protect the young plants from elements such as hail, wind, and frost. We made sure that when the fruit or vegetables were being formed they didn't disconnect from the vine and that the vine didn't disconnect from the roots. If we were careful and diligent, we produced a good crop. And it always made my father proud.

All of us are planting something in our lives every single day, whether we realize it or not. And we are also reaping whatever we have planted in the past. The quality of our lives right now is the result of what we planted and harvested some time before. We reap the good and the bad for years after we have sown. That's why it is so important to plant and nurture the right seeds now.

Jesus said that He is the vine and you and I are the branches. If we abide in Him we will bear fruit (John 15:5). "Abide" means to remain, to stay, to dwell. In other words, if we dwell with Him and He dwells with us, we will bear the fruit of His Spirit (Galatians 5:22-23). That's what we want.

It is said that we begin to resemble the person with whom we live and with whom we are most closely associated. When we share our lives with Jesus, His likeness is stamped on our spirit and soul. When we plug into Him, the fruit of His Spirit is manifested in us.

Nine Good Ways to Produce a Great Crop

1. *Plant seeds of love.* Ask God to plant His love in you in such a profound and powerful way that you are able to fully experience it. Ask also that His love will flow through you to others. Jesus said, "If you keep My commandments, you will abide in My love, just as I have kept My Father's commandments and abide in His love" (John 15:10). Ask God to help you obey all of His laws so that nothing will keep the fullness of His love from blossoming in You.

2. *Plant seeds of joy.* Joy has nothing to do with your circumstances. You can have joy in spite of difficult and painful problems, because joy comes through a close, intimate relationship with the Lord. You can't have joy if you

feel separated from God or don't trust His promises to you. Jesus said, "These things I have spoken to you, that My joy may remain in you, and that your joy may be full" (John 15:11). When you live in the joy of the Lord, you have expectations that God is going to do something great in your life. Pray for the joy of the Lord to be so planted *in* you and manifested *through* you that the crop you reap will spread like wildfire and overtake the fields around you.

3. *Plant seeds of peace.* Pray that the presence of the Lord planted in your life will provide peace that is beyond comprehension. Pray that this peace will grow strong and prevail no matter what your circumstances are. "The peace of God, which surpasses all understanding, will guard your hearts and minds through Christ Jesus" (Philippians 4:7). We can only have true peace if we live in right relationship to God. Pray that God will help you to know His peace in such a powerful way that it brings peace to those around you.

4. *Plant seeds of patience.* Why do you think it's important to God that patience be growing in us? It's because God's timing is not our timing. He is always doing more than we see or know, so we have to trust Him on how long He takes to bring things to pass. God perfects and refines us before He brings us into all He has for us, and that takes time. "Do not become sluggish, but imitate those who through faith and patience inherit the promises" (Hebrews 6:12). "Let patience have its perfect work, that you may be perfect and complete, lacking nothing" (James 1:4). "By your patience possess your souls" (Luke 21:19). Another word for patience is longsuffering. And that says it all. When you suffer for a long time, it means you put up with more than you want to. Pray for God's patience to so be established in your soul that nothing you have to put up with will ever uproot it.

5. *Plant seeds of kindness.* You have a choice in what you plant in a garden. You take the seeds you want and put them in the soil, and God makes them grow. Kindness is something you have to deliberately plant. Or, to put it another way, kindness is something you choose to put on, like a garment. "Therefore, as the elect of God, holy and beloved, put on tender mercies, kindness, humility, meekness, longsuffering" (Colossians 3:12). The ultimate act of kindness was when Jesus gave His life for us. Pray that His brand of kindness will grow in you so that you can lay down your life for others with acts of kindness too.

6. *Plant seeds of goodness.* When the goodness of God is sown in your soul, it leads you to produce good deeds. "A good man out of the good treasure of his heart brings forth good things, and an evil man out of the evil treasure brings forth evil things" (Matthew 12:35). "Every good tree bears good fruit, but a bad tree bears bad fruit. A good tree cannot bear bad fruit, nor can a bad tree bear good fruit" (Matthew 7:17-18). Ask God to help you abide in Him so that His goodness will grow in you. As it grows in your heart, good things will automatically come forth from your life.

7. *Plant seeds of faithfulness.* When we are solid, steadfast, dependable, reliable, loyal, and trustworthy and do what is right no matter what, we exhibit faithfulness. "He who is faithful in what is least is faithful also in much; and he who is unjust in what is least is unjust also in much" (Luke 16:10). Pray that His faithfulness will continually grow strong in you every day that you are alive. Pray that your faithfulness will strengthen everyone you touch and inspire others to greater faithfulness too.

8. *Plant seeds of gentleness.* When we are brash and arrogant, it makes people feel bad about us and bad about themselves. Gentleness is a humble meekness that is calm,

soothing, peaceful, and easy to be around. The Bible says, "a servant of the Lord must not quarrel but be gentle to all" (2 Timothy 2:24). "The wisdom that is from above is first pure, then peaceable, gentle, willing to yield, full of mercy and good fruits, without partiality and without hypocrisy" (James 3:17). Being considerate of the feelings and needs of others by exhibiting gentleness shows you are responding to the Spirit of God and what has been planted in you has taken root. Pray that you can be as gentle and meek as Jesus was (2 Corinthians 10:1).

9. *Plant seeds of self-control.* Self-control is not fragile like a strawberry plant; it's big and solid like an apple tree. Only God can plant something of that magnitude in you and make it bear fruit. Having no self-control means you do whatever pleases you no matter what the consequences are. Pray that you will not be powerless against the forces that tug on your soul. "Add to your faith virtue, to virtue knowledge, to knowledge self-control, to self-control perseverance, to perseverance godliness" (2 Peter 1:5-6). Ask God to plant self-control in you that will grow up like a tree of strength. Ask Him to help you to rein in your passions, desires, and emotions and make them subject to His Spirit. He will give you the self-discipline you need.

If you've not been bearing the fruit of the Spirit in your life the way you'd like, ask God to help you plant good seeds and pull up any weeds that may have grown up around your soul. Feed the soil of your heart with the food of God's Word and ask the Holy Spirit to water it afresh every day. As long as you abide faithfully in the true vine, I guarantee you'll produce a crop of spiritual fruit that will make your heavenly Father proud.

My Prayer to God

Lord, search my heart and try me and see if there is any wickedness in me. Replace all that is wrong in my character with the goodness in Yours. Plant the fruit of Your Spirit in me and cause it to flourish. Help me to abide in You, Jesus, so that I will bear fruit in my life. I invite You, Holy Spirit, to fill me afresh with Your *love* today so that it will flow out of me and into the lives of others.

You said in Your Word to "let the peace of Christ rule in your hearts" (Colossians 3:15). I pray that Your *peace* would rule my heart and mind to such a degree that people would sense it when they are around me. Help me to "pursue the things which make for peace and the things by which one may edify another" (Romans 14:19).

Give me the *joy* that knowing You produces. Make me *patient* with others so that I reflect Your character to them. Help me to be *kind* whenever there is opportunity for it, and may Your *goodness* flow through me so that I will do good to everyone. Make me to be a *faithful* person so that I can be trusted in all things. Help me to have the "meekness and gentleness of Christ" so that I will reflect Your *gentle* spirit (2 Corinthians 10:1). Enable me to be *self-controlled* in my thoughts, words, and habits.

Where I need to be pruned in order to bear more fruit, I submit myself to You. I know that without You I can do nothing. You are the vine and I am the branch. I must abide in You in order to bear fruit. Help me to do that. Thank You for Your promise that if I abide in You and Your Word abides in me, I can ask what I desire and it will be done for me (John 15:7). Thank You for Your promise that says if I ask I will receive (John 16:24). May I be like a tree planted by the rivers of Your living water so that I will bring forth fruit in season that won't wither (Psalm 1:3). In Jesus' name, I ask that the fruit of Your Spirit will grow in me and be recognized clearly by all who see me so that it glorifies You.

GOD'S PROMISES TO ME

The fruit of the Spirit is love, joy, peace, longsuffering, kindness, goodness, faithfulness, gentleness, self-control. Against such there is no law.

GALATIANS 5:22-23

I am the true vine, and My Father is the vinedresser. Every branch in Me that does not bear fruit He takes away; and every branch that bears fruit He prunes, that it may bear more fruit. You are already clean because of the word which I have spoken to you. Abide in Me, and I in you. As the branch cannot bear fruit of itself, unless it abides in the vine, neither can you, unless you abide in Me. I am the vine, you are the branches. He who abides in Me, and I in him, bears much fruit; for without Me you can do nothing. If anyone does not abide in Me, he is cast out as a branch and is withered; and they gather them and throw them into the fire, and they are burned. If you abide in Me, and My words abide in you, you will ask what you desire, and it shall be done for you. By this My Father is glorified, that you bear much fruit; so you will be My disciples.

JOHN 15:1-8

Chapter Thirteen

Lord, Preserve Me in Purity and Holiness

Don't let the title of this chapter intimidate you. Being holy is not being perfect. It's letting *Him* who is holy be *in* you. We can't be holy on our own, but we can make choices that allow holiness and purity to be manifested in our lives. We can separate ourselves from that which dilutes God's holiness in us and die to our lusts. And we are able to do this because "those who are Christ's have crucified the flesh with its passions and desires" (Galatians 5:24). We are not slaves to our flesh. We are able to live pure lives consecrated to the Lord.

You may have heard people say, "I can't tell you exactly what pornography is, but I know it when I see it." Well, the opposite is true for holiness and purity. You may not be able to describe exactly what holiness is, but you know it when you *don't* see it. Here are seven descriptions of what holiness is and how to know when you don't see it in yourself.

Seven Good Ways to Live in Holiness

1. *Holiness means separating yourself from the world.* This doesn't mean you head for the hills, isolate yourself, and

never speak to another nonbeliever. It means your heart detaches from the world's value system. You, instead, value the things God values above all else. The consequences for not doing so are serious. "Do you not know that friendship with the world is enmity with God? Whoever therefore wants to be a friend of the world makes himself an enemy of God" (James 4:4). Who wants to be God's enemy?

I know it's hard to be separate from the world when you live in it. But if that is the desire of your heart, you can ask God to help you do it. Of course, you have to make choices to turn off certain TV programs, not go to certain movies, not read certain magazines, and not frequent certain places. "Do not love the world or the things in the world. If anyone loves the world, the love of the Father is not in him. For all that is in the world—the lust of the flesh, the lust of the eyes, and the pride of life—is not of the Father but is of the world" (1 John 2:15-16). Ask God to help you separate yourself from the things of the world, and learn to love *Him* more than you love *it*.

2. *Holiness means purifying yourself*. Purifying yourself does not mean putting on a white robe to cover up all that is not holy about you. It means asking God, who is holy, to purify your heart. Unholiness happens there first. Purifying ourselves means taking stock of our lives, thoughts, actions, associations, and business dealings, and cleansing ourselves from anything that contaminates us. It is something we *actively* do. It means deciding to be morally and ethically pure. "Everyone who has this hope in Him purifies himself, just as He is pure" (1 John 3:3).

When God said, "Be holy" (Leviticus 19:2), the commands He gave following that had to do with not stealing, not lying, not committing fraud, not slandering people, not trying to get revenge, and not falling into idolatry. It means that we are to take specific steps to see that we do not live an impure lifestyle. We are to deliberately turn away from anything that glorifies immorality and other unholiness. "As He who called you is holy, you also be holy in all your conduct, because it is written, 'Be holy, for I am holy'" (1 Peter 1:15-16). Pray that you will be able to thoroughly search out and examine your ways, and turn to the Lord (Lamentations 3:40).

3. *Holiness means living in the Spirit and not in the flesh.* Our fleshly thoughts will disqualify us as much as our actions. Are we jealous of anyone? Do we have strife? Is there unresolved division in our lives? Do we willfully allow sin a place? If so, then we are living in the flesh. And it will destroy us. "For those who live according to the flesh set their minds on the things of the flesh, but those who live according to the Spirit, the things of the Spirit. For to be carnally minded is death, but to be spiritually minded is life and peace. Because the carnal mind is enmity against God; for it is not subject to the law of God, nor indeed can be. So then, those who are in the flesh cannot please God" (Romans 8:5-8).

When you look honestly at the fruit of your life, you can see by what you are reaping whether you have sown to the flesh or to the Spirit. "Do not be deceived, God is not mocked; for whatever a man sows, that he will also reap. For he who sows to his flesh will of the flesh reap corruption, but he who sows to the Spirit will of the Spirit reap everlasting life" (Galatians 6:7-8). Pray that God will help you live in the Spirit and not the flesh.

4. *Holiness means staying clear of sexual immorality.* The greatest lie our society has blindly accepted is that sexual sin is okay. It must grieve the Holy Spirit to see how women sell themselves short of all God has for them because they have

bought into this lie. For example, a self-deceived generation believes that oral sex with someone they aren't married to is not actually sex at all, so therefore they can indulge their flesh and not reap any consequences. "There is a generation that is pure in its own eyes, yet is not washed from its filthiness" (Proverbs 30:12). While they may be safe from conceiving a baby, they will conceive death in their souls and then wonder why after they are married the passion in their marriage dies. Holiness means not falling prey to fashion or trends of thought or deed. "For this is the will of God, your sanctification: that you should abstain from sexual immorality; that each of you should know how to possess his own vessel in sanctification and honor, not in passion of lust, like the Gentiles who do not know God" (1 Thessalonians 4:3-5). Ask God to keep you sexually pure in your mind, soul, and body.

5. *Holiness means being sanctified by Jesus.* Once we have received Jesus, we can't continue to live our old sinful lifestyle. Now that we have Him living in us and the Holy Spirit filling us and transforming us, we have no excuse. "We have been sanctified through the offering of the body of Jesus Christ once for all" (Hebrews 10:10). "For by one offering He has perfected forever those who are being sanctified" (Hebrews 10:14). This doesn't mean we don't have to be concerned about sin anymore and can do whatever we want because He took care of it. It means we must *continue* to dwell with Him and ask God to help us live in all He bought for us on the cross.

6. *Holiness means walking close to God.* When we do not pursue a close walk with God and a lifestyle of purity and peace, we are unable to see the Lord with any kind of clarity. "Pursue peace with all people, and holiness, without which no one will see the Lord" (Hebrews 12:14). Esteeming the

holiness of God and living in purity is the only way we are able to be close to Him. "Who may ascend into the hill of the LORD? Or who may stand in His holy place? He who has clean hands and a pure heart, who has not lifted up his soul to an idol, nor sworn deceitfully" (Psalm 24:3-4). "By those who come near Me I must be regarded as holy; and before all the people I must be glorified" (Leviticus 10:3). There is nothing more important than being close to God.

There comes a time in all of our lives when we are *desperate* to know that God is close and that He hears our prayers and will answer. We won't have time to *get* right with God; we will have to *be* right with God. "The LORD has set apart for Himself him who is godly; the LORD will hear when I call to Him" (Psalm 4:3). Now is the time to start living righteous, pure, and holy lives if we want to see our prayers answered in the future.

7. *Holiness means letting God keep you.* Holiness is not something you slip in and out of like a nightgown. Holiness is God's will for our lives, and something God has planned for us from the beginning. "Just as He chose us in Him before the foundation of the world, that we should be holy and without blame before Him in love, having predestined us to adoption as sons by Jesus Christ to Himself, according to the good pleasure of His will" (Ephesians 1:4-5). God has made a way for us to live in holiness. And He is able to *keep* us holy. When our heart wants to live in purity and do the right thing, God will keep us from falling into sin.

When Abraham told King Abimelech that Sarah was his sister instead of telling him that she was his wife, Abimelech took her into his own house. But in a dream God told Abimelech that he would soon be a dead man because he had taken another man's wife. Abimelech said, "In the integrity of my heart and innocence of my hands I have done this" (Genesis 20:5).

God replied to Abimelech, "Yes, I know that you did this in the integrity of your heart. For I also withheld you from sinning against Me; therefore I did not let you touch her" (Genesis 20:6).

When we live right, God will *keep* us from sin.

It is only by the grace of God that we can live in holiness, even after we have chosen to do so. That's because God enables us to do what He asks us to do. But we still need to *ask* Him to do it. God wants to know that His holiness is important enough to us to seek after it. People are drawn to holiness because it is attractive, even though they may resist it in their own lives. Ask God to enhance your beauty with the beauty of His holiness.

My Prayer to God

Lord, You have said in Your Word that You did not call me to uncleanness, but in holiness (1 Thessalonians 4:7). You chose me to be holy and blameless before You. I know that I have been washed clean and made holy by the blood of Jesus (1 Corinthians 6:11). You have clothed me in Your righteousness and enabled me to put on the new man "in true righteousness and holiness" (Ephesians 4:24). Continue to purify me by the power of Your Spirit. Help me to "cling to what is good" (Romans 12:9) and keep myself pure (1 Timothy 5:22).

Lord, help me to separate myself from anything that is not holy. I don't want to waste my life on things that have no value. Give me discernment to recognize that which is worthless and remove myself from it. Help me not to give myself to impure things, but rather to those things that fulfill Your plans for my life. Enable me to do what it takes to get everything rooted out of my life that is not Your best for me, so I can live the way You want me to live. Show me how to tear down any idols in my life and eliminate any sources of unholy thoughts, such as TV, movies, books, videos, and magazines, that do not glorify You. Help me to examine my ways so that I can return to Your ways wherever I have strayed. Enable me to take any steps necessary in order to be pure before You.

Lord, I want to be holy as You are holy. Make me a partaker of Your holiness (Hebrews 12:10), and may my spirit, soul, and body be kept blameless (1 Thessalonians 5:23). I know that You have called me to purity and holiness and You have said that "He who calls you is faithful, who will also do it" (1 Thessalonians 5:24). Thank You that You will keep me pure and holy so I will be fully prepared for all You have for me.

God's Promises to Me

He chose us in Him before the foundation of the world, that we should be holy and without blame before Him in love.
Ephesians 1:4

Blessed are the pure in heart, for they shall see God.
Matthew 5:8

In a great house there are not only vessels of gold and silver, but also of wood and clay, some for honor and some for dishonor. Therefore if anyone cleanses

himself from the latter, he will be a vessel for honor,
sanctified and useful for the Master,
prepared for every good work.

2 Timothy 2:20-21

Therefore, having these promises, beloved, let us cleanse ourselves from all filthiness of the flesh and spirit, perfecting holiness in the fear of God.

2 Corinthians 7:1

A highway shall be there, and a road, and it shall be called the Highway of Holiness. The unclean shall not pass over it, but it shall be for others. Whoever walks the road, although a fool, shall not go astray. No lion shall be there, nor shall any ravenous beast go up on it; it shall not be found there. But the redeemed shall walk there. And the ransomed of the Lord shall return, and come to Zion with singing, with everlasting joy on their heads. They shall obtain joy and gladness, and sorrow and sighing shall flee away.

Isaiah 35:8-10

Chapter Fourteen

Lord, Move Me into the Purpose for Which I Was Created

When my children were growing up, I frequently prayed they would have a sense of who God made them to be and what their purpose was. I had observed so many young people floundering around and wasting their lives because they had no idea they were called to something great in the Lord. I had done the same thing when I was young, and I ended up in serious trouble. I certainly wanted more than that for my children. As a result of those prayers, I have never seen my children without a sense of purpose. Now that they are in their 20s, they continue to move in their gifts and their paths are becoming more and more clear. They don't know the exact details of their future, but they each know that they have one and that it is good.

When I wrote *The Power of a Praying® Parent* and shared my many years of experiences in praying for children, I received a large volume of mail from people telling me how they wished they'd had someone praying for them like that when they were growing up. They now feared they had wasted too many years trying to figure out what they were supposed to be doing and missed the purpose God had for their lives. I encouraged them with this good news. "No matter how far off the path you have gotten from the plans and purposes God has for you, when you surrender your life to the Lord and declare your utter dependence upon Him, He carves a path from where you are to where you are supposed to be, and He sets you on it. It may take you longer than it would have taken had you been on the right path from the beginning, but if you keep walking closely with God, He will get you where you are supposed to be."

Don't ever think it's too late for you. The Bible says, "The gifts and the calling of God are irrevocable" (Romans 11:29). That means the gifts and abilities He gives to you He doesn't take back. They won't be recalled, repealed, or annulled. You will always have your gifts. However, this is not true of the anointing. The anointing is the presence and touch of God upon your gifts that gives them supernatural power to penetrate darkness and bring life and light. This spiritual touch of the Holy Spirit can be lost through sin without repentance. We've all seen people who have fallen into immorality, yet they kept on using their gifts without recognizing that the anointing was gone. They had been so deceived and their sin had so blinded them that they didn't even realize what it was they had lost.

Everyone Has a Purpose

Each one of us has a purpose in the Lord. But many of us don't realize that. And when we don't have an accurate understanding of our identity, we either strive to be like someone else or something we're not. We compare ourselves to others and feel as though we always fall short.

When we don't become who *we* think we're *supposed* to be, it makes us critical of ourselves and our lives. It causes us to be insecure, oversensitive, judgmental, frustrated, and unfulfilled. We become self-absorbed, constantly having to think about ourselves and what we *should* be. It forces us to try too hard to make life happen the way we think it is supposed to. In the extreme, it makes us tell lies about ourselves and become dishonest about who we really are. When you are around people who don't have any idea of what they are called to do, you sense their unrest, unfulfillment, anxiety, and lack of peace.

God doesn't want that for you. He wants you to have a clear vision for your life. He wants to reveal to you what your gifts and talents are and show you how to best develop them and use them for His glory.

Know Who You Are and Where You Are Going

Predestination means your destination has already been determined. The Bible says we are predestined according to God's purposes and will (Ephesians 1:11). That means God knows where you are supposed to be going. And He knows how to get you there. But even though you have a purpose and a destiny, you can't get to it without being connected to the one who gave it to you in the first place. When you don't stay connected to the one who planned your destiny, then in one moment of weakness, such as passion or anger, you can sell it out. We see people on the news all the time who do that. When you clearly understand that God has a high purpose for your life, you won't throw it away with a foolish decision. You won't allow insecurity to ruin your life.

It doesn't seem fair that insecurity is sin. That's like hitting someone when they are down. But insecurity is a lack of faith. And a lack of faith is sin, because it signifies a lack of trust in God. When we are insecure about who we are and what our purpose is, it means we don't trust God with our lives. We don't believe that what He says about us in His word is true. Insecurity causes us to focus on ourselves and what *we* want, instead of focusing on Him and what *He* wants.

We all want to accomplish something significant with our lives. And we all have the potential to do something great. That's because we are the Lord's and His Spirit dwells in us. Because of His greatness *in* us, He can accomplish great things *through* us. We just have to remember not to confuse success in the eyes of men as being the same as success in the eyes of God. Men and women of the world glory in their accomplishments. Children of God glory in the Lord. "Let not the wise man glory in his wisdom, let not the mighty man glory in his might, nor let the rich man glory in his riches; but let him who glories glory in this, that he understands and knows Me" (Jeremiah 9:23-24). When you know you are the Lord's and you trust where He is taking you, you feel very secure.

Surrender Your Dreams

I have found that we can never move into all God has for us and become all He created us to be without surrendering our dreams to Him. Jesus said, "Whoever desires to save his life will lose it, but whoever loses his life for My sake will find it" (Matthew 16:25). That means if we want to have a life that is secure in the Lord, we have to let go of *our* plans and say, "Not my will, but *Yours* be done, Lord." This is hard to do, because letting go of our dreams is the last thing we want to do. But we have to ask Him to take away the dreams in our heart that are not of Him and bring to pass the ones that are.

If you have a dream that is not of God, when you surrender it to Him He will take away your desire for it and give you what *He* has for you. This can be very painful, especially if it is a dream you've been clinging to for a long time. But you don't want to spend your life chasing after a dream that God will not bless. You will be constantly frustrated if you do, and it will never be realized. You want to be living the dreams God puts in your heart.

Even if the dreams you have in your heart are from God, you will still have to surrender them. That's because God wants you clinging to *Him* and not to your dreams. He doesn't want you trying to make them happen. He wants you to trust *Him*, and *He'll* make them happen.

Finding Your Purpose

We all need to have a sense of why we are here. We all need to know we were created for a purpose. We will never find fulfillment and happiness until we are doing the thing for which we were created. But God won't move us into the big things He has called us to unless we have been proven faithful in the small things He has given us. So if you are doing what you deem to be small things right now, rejoice! God's getting you ready for big things ahead.

Don't think for a moment that if you haven't moved into the purposes God has for you by now that it's too late. It is *never* too late. I did everything late. I didn't come to the Lord until I was 28. I got married late, had children late, and didn't even start writing professionally until I was over 40. My whole ministry happened when I was in my 40s and most of it in my 50s. Trust me, if you are still breathing, God has a purpose for you. He has something for you to do *now*.

If you are not sure what God wants you to do, start as an intercessor. We are all called to pray for others. Start by serving in your church. We are all called to submit ourselves to a body of believers and help others. When we are faithful in these things, He moves us into others.

Keep in mind that God "has saved us and called us with a holy calling, not according to our works, but according to His own purpose and grace which was given to us in Christ Jesus before time began" (2 Timothy 1:9). "Having then gifts differing according to the grace that is given to us, let us use them" (Romans 12:6). For "each one has his own gift from God, one in this manner and another in that" (1 Corinthians 7:7). So then, "as God has distributed to each one, as the Lord has called each one, so let him walk" (1 Corinthians 7:17).

I pray that God will "give to you the spirit of wisdom and revelation in the knowledge of Him, the eyes of your understanding being enlightened; that you may know what is the hope of His calling" (Ephesians 1:17-18). "May He grant you according to your heart's desire, and fulfill all your purpose" (Psalm 20:4).

May you never forget, dear sister, that God has an important purpose for your life and that it is good.

My Prayer to God

Lord, I thank You that You have called me with a holy calling, not according to my works, but according to Your purpose and grace which was given to me in Christ Jesus (2 Timothy 1:9). I know that Your plan for me existed before I knew You, and You will bring it to pass. Help me to "walk worthy of the calling with which [I was] called" (Ephesians 4:1). I know there is an appointed plan for me, and I have a destiny that will now be fulfilled.

Help me to live my life with a sense of purpose and understanding of the calling You have given me. I lay down all pride, selfishness, and anything else that would keep me from moving into all You have for me. I don't want to miss out on Your full purpose for my life because I did not walk the way You wanted me to. I repent of every day I haven't fully lived for You. Help me to live the way You want me to from now on.

Lord, help me to understand the call You have on my life. Take away any discouragement I may feel and replace it with joyful anticipation of what You are going to do through me. Use me as Your instrument to make a positive difference in the lives of those whom You put in my path. Help me to rest in the confidence of knowing that Your timing is perfect. I know that whatever You have called me to do, You will enable me to do it.

I pray that nothing will draw me away from fulfilling the plan You have for me. May I never stray from what You have called me to be and do. Give me a vision for my life and a strong sense of purpose. I put my identity in You and my destiny in Your hands. Show me if what I am doing now is what I am supposed to be doing. I want what You are building in my life to last for eternity. I don't want to waste time going after things that are not what You have for me. Help me to be content where I am, knowing You won't leave me there forever.

Lord, I know that "all things work together for good" to those who love You and are called according to Your purpose (Romans 8:28). I don't want to presume that I know what that purpose is. Nor do I want to spend a lifetime trying to figure out what I am supposed to be doing and miss the mark.

So I pray that You would show me clearly what the gifts and talents are that You have placed in me. Lead me in the way I should go as I grow in them. Enable me to use them according to Your will and for Your glory.

God's Promises to Me

Walk worthy of the calling with which you were called, with all lowliness and gentleness, with longsuffering, bearing with one another in love, endeavoring to keep the unity of the Spirit in the bond of peace.
Ephesians 4:1-3

Be even more diligent to make your call and election sure, for if you do these things you will never stumble.
2 Peter 1:10

You are a chosen generation, a royal priesthood, a holy nation, His own special people, that you may proclaim the praises of Him who called you out of darkness into His marvelous light.
1 Peter 2:9

In Him also we have obtained an inheritance, being predestined according to the purpose of Him who works all things according to the counsel of His will, that we who first trusted in Christ should be to the praise of His glory.
Ephesians 1:11-12

Whom He predestined, these He also called; whom He called, these He also justified; and whom He justified, these He also glorified.
Romans 8:30

Chapter Fifteen

Lord, Guide Me in All My Relationships

I once heard a radio interview with some gang members in Los Angeles. At the time crime was extremely high in that city due to a terrifying wave of random drive-by shootings and murders perpetrated by gang members. These boys—some barely teenagers and some in their early 20s—said the main reason they joined their gang was to have a sense of belonging. In a chilling statement a number of them admitted they would do whatever it took to ensure they were accepted and esteemed by the group. Even commit murder.

Some of the boys revealed that the test of whether they could even be accepted into the gang was to go out and kill someone. There was no other reason for the murder other than to complete the initiation requirement and prove that they would do anything for the group. Some confessed how much they hated doing it and wished there had been another alternative. But they were desperate to belong to a family, so they went ahead with it. This was a frightening revelation to all of us who lived there, because it meant no place was safe.

Around that same time, a friend of ours was out in front of his own home in broad daylight and was approached by two such young boys. They were walking down the street, which was in a very nice and quiet residential neighborhood, when one of the boys pulled out a gun, shot our friend point-blank and fled. There was no robbery or attempt to commit any other crime. Our friend must have had angels watching over him, because he lived through it. Most people involved in such incidents didn't. But the damage to his body greatly affected his ability to do the work he was an expert in doing, and it took him years to recover.

These young boys in the interview had no sense of purpose for their lives outside of belonging to a gang. Most of them were raised without fathers and in some cases the mother was absent too. I'm sure that if each of them would have had a strong sense of family, and love and acceptance from other people, they would not have chosen this destructive lifestyle. This illustrates how desperately people need people. When young people are deprived of good, godly relationships, they will seek those that aren't. That's how gangs are formed.

We *all* desperately need a sense of family, of relationship, of belonging. If you don't realize that about yourself, it's probably because you have always had it. God created us to be in families. We have a natural hunger to be a part of something that gives us a sense of acceptance, affirmation, and being needed and appreciated. But even if we have never received that from our own biological families, there is good news. God sets us in *spiritual* families. In many ways these can be just as important.

The Importance of Having a Spiritual Family

God is our Father. We are God's kids. That means we who are believers in Jesus are all brothers and sisters. There are too many of us to all live in the same house, so God puts us in separate houses. We call them churches. Our relationships within these church families are crucial to our well-being. How we relate to the other people there will greatly affect the quality of our life in the Lord. We can never reach our full destiny apart from the people God puts in our lives. I don't mean they will necessarily help us do what we do, but our relationships with them will contribute to our success.

It's important to be yoked with people who walk closely with God. Accountability results from having close relationships with strong believers who are themselves accountable to other strong believers. It's important to be accountable because we are all capable of being deceived. We all have blind spots. We need people who will help us see the truth about ourselves and our lives. And we need to have the kind of relationships that don't break down when truth is spoken in love.

This doesn't mean that you will never have a problem in any of your church relationships or that if you do it's a sign that you are in the wrong place. *All* relationships have things that need to be worked out. Getting beyond those problems are what make relationships rich. But we have to learn to protect our relationships with our spiritual family in prayer.

Your enemy doesn't want you to be in a spiritual family or have godly relationships. That's because he knows how beneficial they are for you. He knows that without a spiritual family you won't grow properly. He knows if you are not joined and committed to a spiritual family, you will end up living in rebellion in some way whether you mean to or not. He knows you will never be all God created you to be if you are not connected to a spiritual family. That's why he will try to break apart your relationships. And that's why you should cover them in prayer.

More Than Just Friends

So much is made of the importance of the right kind of friends in the Bible that we can't treat this part of our lives lightly. "The righteous should choose his friends carefully, for the way of the wicked leads them astray" (Proverbs 12:26). If it's true that we become like the friends we spend time with, then we must select our friends wisely. The main quality to look for in a close friend is not how attractive, talented, wealthy, smart, influential, clever, or popular they are. It's how much they love and fear God. The person who will do what it takes to live in the perfect will of God is the kind of friend who imparts something of the goodness of the Lord to you every time you are with them.

God doesn't want us to be unequally yoked with unbelievers, but that doesn't mean we should have nothing to do with anyone who doesn't know the Lord. Far from it. We are God's tool to reach others for His kingdom. But our closest relationships, the ones that influence us the most, need to be with people who love and fear God. If you don't have close friends who are believers, pray for godly and desirable friends to come into your life.

Seven Good Signs of a Desirable Friend

1. *A desirable friend tells you the truth in love.* "Faithful are the wounds of a friend, but the kisses of an enemy are deceitful" (Proverbs 27:6).

2. *A desirable friend gives you sound advice.* "Ointment and perfume delight the heart, and the sweetness of a man's friend gives delight by hearty counsel" (Proverbs 27:9).

3. A *desirable friend refines you.* "As iron sharpens iron, so a man sharpens the countenance of his friend" (Proverbs 27:17).

4. A *desirable friend helps you grow in wisdom.* "He who walks with wise men will be wise, but the companion of fools will be destroyed" (Proverbs 13:20).

5. A *desirable friend stays close to you.* "A man who has friends must himself be friendly, but there is a friend who sticks closer than a brother" (Proverbs 18:24).

6. A *desirable friend loves you and stands by you.* "A friend loves at all times, and a brother is born for adversity" (Proverbs 17:17).

7. A *desirable friend is a help in time of trouble.* "Two are better than one, because they have a good reward for their labor. For if they fall, one will lift up his companion. But woe to him who is alone when he falls, for he has no one to help him up" (Ecclesiastes 4:9-10).

If you have friends with these qualities, protect those friendships with prayer. If you have friends who have less than desirable qualities, you need to pray about those as well.

Seven Signs of an *Undesirable* Friend

1. An *undesirable friend is immoral and has no regard for others.* "I have written to you not to keep company with anyone named a brother, who is sexually immoral, or covetous, or an idolater, or a reviler, or a drunkard, or an extortioner—not even to eat with such a person" (1 Corinthians 5:11).

2. An *undesirable friend is changeable and unstable.* "Do not associate with those given to change; for their calamity will rise suddenly, and who knows the ruin those two can bring?" (Proverbs 24:21-22).

3. *An undesirable friend is frequently angry.* "Make no friendship with an angry man, and with a furious man do not go, lest you learn his ways and set a snare for your soul" (Proverbs 22:24-25).

4. *An undesirable friend gives ungodly counsel.* "Blessed is the man who walks not in the counsel of the ungodly, nor stands in the path of sinners, nor sits in the seat of the scornful" (Psalm 1:1).

5. *An undesirable friend is a lawless unbeliever.* "Do not be unequally yoked together with unbelievers. For what fellowship has righteousness with lawlessness? And what communion has light with darkness? And what accord has Christ with Belial? Or what part has a believer with an unbeliever?" (2 Corinthians 6:14-15).

6. *An undesirable friend is a fool.* "He who walks with wise men will be wise, but the companion of fools will be destroyed" (Proverbs 13:20).

7. *An undesirable friend is irreverent toward God and His laws.* "I am a companion of all who fear You, and of those who keep Your precepts" (Psalm 119:63).

If you have friends with such characteristics as these, ask God to send you new friends while you pray for the old ones to be transformed.

Pray for Your Relationships

Severe injuries to relationships can often be fatal. Even if they aren't completely destroyed, relational injuries can take years to heal. It's easier to *protect* them in prayer than it is to *fix* them. The way we learned to cope, survive, or interact in our relationships when we were growing up will be carried with us into adulthood and affect every one of our important or close relationships now. And it could be exactly how the devil will try to destroy them. Ask God to make you a good friend to others and give you a pure and loving heart in all your relationships. Pray especially for the people you live with. The Bible says that "every...house divided against itself will not stand" (Matthew 12:25). You can't have peace if you are living in discord with anyone in your home.

Don't leave your relationships to chance. Pray for godly people to come into your life with whom you can connect. Don't *force* relationships to happen, *pray* for them to happen. Then when they do, nurture them with prayer. This doesn't mean you have to have large numbers of friends. There is great strength in small numbers when the people involved are strong in the Lord. The quality of your relationships is more important than the quantity.

Throughout your whole life relationships will be crucial to your well-being. It is not emotionally or spiritually healthy to be isolated. Right relationships will enrich and balance you and give you a healthy perspective. Godly people will help you walk in the right direction, and the good in them will rub off on you. The quality of your relationships will determine the quality of your life. And this is something worth praying about.

My Prayer to God

Lord, I lift up every one of my relationships to You and ask You to bless them. I pray that each one would be glorifying to You. Help me to choose my friends wisely so I won't be led astray. Give me discernment and strength to separate myself from anyone who is not a good influence. I release all my relationships to You and pray that Your will be done in each one of them.

With my most difficult relationships, I ask that Your peace would reign in them. Specifically I lift up to You my relationship with (name a difficult friend). I know two can't walk together unless they are agreed (Amos 3:3), so help us to find a place of agreement, unity, and like-mindedness. Where either of us needs to change, I pray that You would change us. Break down any "wall of separation" (Ephesians 2:13-15) or misunderstanding. I release this person into Your hands and ask that You would make our relationship what You want it to be so that it will glorify You.

I pray for my relationship with each of my family members. Specifically, I pray for my relationship with (name the family member with whom you are most concerned). I pray You would bring healing, reconciliation, and restoration where it is needed. Bless our relationship and make it strong.

I pray for any relationships I have with people who don't know You, Lord. Give me words to say that will turn their hearts toward You. Help me to be Your light to them. Specifically I pray for (name an unbeliever or someone who has walked away from God). Soften this person's heart to open her (his) eyes to receive You and follow You faithfully.

I pray for godly friends, role models, and mentors to come into my life. Send people who will speak the truth in love. I pray especially that there will be women in my life who are trustworthy, kind, loving, and faithful. Most of all I pray that they be women of strong faith who will add to my life and I to theirs. May we mutually raise the standards to which we aspire. May forgiveness and love flow freely between us. Make me to be Your light in all my relationships.

God's Promises to Me

You are no longer strangers and foreigners, but fellow citizens with the saints and members of the household of God, having been built on the foundation of the apostles and prophets, Jesus Christ Himself being the chief cornerstone, in whom the whole building, being joined together, grows into a holy temple in the Lord, in whom you also are being built together for a dwelling place of God in the Spirit.

Ephesians 2:19-22

God sets the solitary in families; He brings out those who are bound into prosperity; but the rebellious dwell in a dry land.

Psalm 68:6

Let all bitterness, wrath, anger, clamor, and evil speaking be put away from you, with all malice. And be kind to one another, tenderhearted, forgiving one another, just as God in Christ forgave you.

Ephesians 4:31-32

We should no longer be children, tossed to and fro and carried about with every wind of doctrine, by the trickery of men, in the cunning craftiness of deceitful plotting, but, speaking the truth in love, may grow up in all things into Him who is the head—Christ—from whom the whole body, joined and knit together by what every joint supplies,

according to the effective working by which every
part does its share, causes growth of the body for
the edifying of itself in love.
EPHESIANS 4:14-16

Chapter Sixteen

Lord, Keep Me in the Center of Your Will

When my children and I walked through the rubble of our house in Northridge, California, not long after the Northridge earthquake of 1993 had destroyed it, we all wept. We knew that if we'd been in the house at the time, we might not have lived through that earthquake. We all loved that great house and had hated to leave it when we moved just months before. A lot of prayer and inner struggle went into the decision to relocate to another state, but we were certain it was God's leading. We had not even sold the house before we moved because we felt we were to leave right away. Had we not sought the will of God for our lives and followed it, even with reluctance, we would have been there when the earthquake happened.

God's will is a place of safety. I'm not saying that anyone who was in California during the earthquake was out of the will of God. But, I believe that *we* would have been. And I believe that the reason the house had not sold is that anyone who was in it at the time would have been seriously injured or killed. When we walk in the will of God, we find safety. When we live outside of God's will, we forfeit His protection.

We all want to be in the center of God's will. That's why we shouldn't pursue a career, a move to another place, or any major life change without the knowledge that it is the will of God. We must regularly ask God to show us what His will is and lead us in it. We must ask Him to speak to our heart so He can tell us. "Your ears shall hear a word behind you, saying, 'This is the way, walk in it,' whenever you turn to the right hand or whenever you turn to the left" (Isaiah 30:21). My family and I will always be grateful that we listened to God and followed His leading.

Four Good Things That Are True About God's Will

1. *Following God's will does not mean we will never have trouble*. Trouble is a part of life. Having fulfillment and peace in the midst of trouble is what living in God's will is all about. There is great confidence in knowing that you are walking in the will of God and doing what He wants you to do. When you are sure of that, you can better deal with what life brings you. So don't think that trouble in your life means you are out of God's will. God uses the trouble you have to perfect you. There is a big difference between being out of God's will and being pruned or tested by God. Both are uncomfortable, but one leads to life and one doesn't. In one you will have peace, no matter how uncomfortable it gets. In the other, you won't.

2. *Following God's will is not easy*. The life of Jesus confirms that following God's will is not always fun, enjoyable, pleasant, and easy. Jesus was doing God's will when He went to the cross. He said, "For I have come down from heaven, not to do My own will, but the will of Him who sent Me" (John 6:38). If anyone could have said, "I don't want to

follow God's will today," I think it would have been Him. But He did it perfectly. And now He will enable us to do it too.

3. *Following God's will can make you very uncomfortable.* In fact, if you don't ever feel stretched or uncomfortable in your walk with the Lord, then I would question whether you are actually *in* the will of God. It has been my personal experience that stretched and uncomfortable is a way of life when walking in the will of God.

4. *Following God's will doesn't happen automatically.* That's because God gave us a choice as to whether we subject our will to Him or not. We make that decision every day. Will we *seek* His will? Will we *ask* Him for wisdom? Will we *do* what He says? "Do not be unwise, but understand what the will of the Lord is" (Ephesians 5:17). God's will is the way we choose to live each day of our lives.

God doesn't want you to live your life for the lusts of the flesh, "but for the will of God" (1 Peter 4:2). He wants to "make you complete in every good work to do His will, working in you what is well pleasing in His sight" (Hebrews 13:21). "For it is God who works in you both to will and to do for His good pleasure" (Philippians 2:13). I pray that in everything you do "you may stand perfect and complete in all the will of God" (Colossians 4:12).

The best place to start seeking God's will for your life is "in everything give thanks; for this is the will of God in Christ Jesus for you" (1 Thessalonians 5:18). Thank Him for keeping you in the center of His will. Then ask Him to guide your every step. It feels so good to be confident you are on the right path and doing what God *wants* that I know you will do whatever it takes to experience it.

My Prayer to God

Lord, I pray You will fill me with the "knowledge of [Your] will in all wisdom and spiritual understanding" (Colossians 1:9). Help me to walk in a worthy manner, fully pleasing to You, being fruitful in every good work and increasing in the knowledge of Your ways. Guide my every step. Lead me "in Your righteousness" and "make Your way straight before my face" (Psalm 5:8). As I draw close and walk in intimate relationship with You each day, I pray You will get me where I need to go.

Even as Jesus said, "Not My will, but Yours, be done" (Luke 22:42), so I say to You, not *my* will but *Your* will be done in my life. "I delight to do Your will, O my God" (Psalm 40:8). You are more important to me than anything. Your will is more important to me than my desires. I want to live as Your servant, doing Your will from my heart (Ephesians 6:6).

Lord, align my heart with Yours. Help me to hear Your voice saying, "This is the way, walk in it." If I am doing anything outside of Your will, show me. Speak to me from Your Word so that I will have understanding. Show me any area of my life where I am not right on target. If there is something I should be doing, reveal it to me so that I can correct my course. I want to do only what You want me to do.

Lord, I know we are not to direct our own steps (Jeremiah 10:23). So I pray *You* would direct my steps. Only You know the way I should go. I don't want to get off the path You want me to walk on and end up in the wrong place. I want to move into all You have for me and become all You made me to be by walking in Your perfect will for my life now.

GOD'S PROMISES TO ME

Not everyone who says to Me, "Lord, Lord," shall enter the kingdom of heaven, but he who does the will of My Father in heaven.
MATTHEW 7:21

You have need of endurance, so that after you have done the will of God,
you may receive the promise.
HEBREWS 10:36

For it is better, if it is the will of God,
to suffer for doing good than for doing evil.
1 PETER 3:17

Therefore let those who suffer according to the will of God commit their souls to Him in doing good, as to a faithful Creator.
1 PETER 4:19

The world is passing away, and the lust of it;
but he who does the will of God abides forever.
1 JOHN 2:17

Chapter Seventeen

Lord, Protect Me and All I Care About

Recently I had the privilege of staying in a high-rise condominium right on the beach. This particular unit was on the top floor, and one entire side of it—which included the bedroom, living room, and dining area—was all glass and overlooked the ocean. The view was breathtaking.

The first morning I awakened there, I opened up the curtains and crawled back into bed to gaze out over the ocean and jot down some thoughts on a notepad. Because the condo was so high, I couldn't see anything but ocean and sky from where I was sitting. In order to have seen the sand of the beach, I would have had to go into the living room and walk out on the balcony to look over the edge.

I was deep in thought, lost in the blue of the sky and ocean, when suddenly a large airplane flew by my window at eye level. It was over the water but it seemed very close. The sudden appearance of something so loud and enormous nearly caused my heart to stop. I felt a surge of panic and fright so severe that it sent a sharp pain throughout my chest. I was terrified by what I saw and shocked at my reaction.

I don't know when I have ever responded so violently to something that was not really a threat. But it was so unexpected, and I had never dreamed of seeing a plane at eye level. I felt utterly vulnerable. I realized at that very moment the only thing standing between me and instant death was the hand of God and a pilot who was a decent human being.

Before September 11, a plane coming in my window was not a thought that would have ever entered my mind. But actually that possibility was always there, whether I realized it or not. I began to wonder about how many other potentially dangerous things are around us every day. Things we don't see until the plans of evil explode them in our lives. Dangers we can't even imagine until they come crashing in upon us, changing us forever.

Personally, I believe our heavenly Father looks out for us and protects us from danger far more than we realize. But it's not something we can take for granted. It's something we must pray about often.

Part of being protected by God has to do with obeying Him and living in His will. When we don't do either of those things, we come out from under the umbrella of His covering. We don't hear His voice telling us which way to go. How many times would people have been spared from something disastrous if they had only asked God to show them what to do and then obeyed Him? Or if they had only just been listening?

I remember traveling one time in my four-wheel-drive vehicle a few days after a freezing snowstorm. Slowly approaching a red light at a busy intersection, I put my foot on the brake but nothing happened. I had hit a patch of black ice that was completely invisible. The intersection consisted of narrow two-lane highways crossing one another, with deep water-drainage ditches on either side. There were cars going both ways across the intersection in front of me, and I realized my car was entirely out of control and I couldn't stop.

"Jesus, help me," I prayed. I tried my best to maintain control over the car and keep it from flipping over into one of the ditches on either side of me. In an effort to do that, however, I spun out in the center of the intersection. Cars dodged all around me as they tried to maintain control as well. One green car was headed directly toward me, and I don't even know how I missed hitting it, except to say that I was praying fervently at the time and the hand of God must have intervened. It was miraculous that nothing happened to me or anyone else. Before I had left home that day, I prayed specifically that God would keep me safe. There is no doubt in my mind that He answered that prayer.

In those precarious moments, when your future is hanging in the balance, you want the confidence of knowing you have been communicating with your heavenly Father all along and He has His eye on you. These are the times, such as what I experienced, when you need a prayer answered instantly. But in order to be sure that happens, you must be praying every day. God is a place of safety you can run to, but it helps if you are running to Him on a daily basis so that you are in familiar territory. The Bible says, "In the fear of the LORD there is strong confidence, and His children will have a place of refuge. The fear of the LORD is a fountain of life, to turn one away from the snares of death" (Proverbs 14:26-27). When we have our eyes on *God*, He keeps an eye on *us*.

My Prayer to God

Lord, I pray for Your hand of protection to be upon me. Keep me safe from any accidents, diseases, or evil influences. Protect me wherever I go. Keep me safe in planes, cars, or any other means of transportation. I trust in Your Word, which assures me that You are my rock, my fortress, my deliverer, my shield, my stronghold, and my strength in whom I trust.

Lord, I want to dwell in Your secret place and abide in Your shadow (Psalm 91:1). Keep me under the umbrella of Your protection. Help me never to stray from the center of Your will or off the path You have for me. Enable me to always hear Your voice guiding me. Send Your angels to keep charge over me and keep me in all my ways. May they bear me up, so that I will not even stumble (Psalm 91:12). You, Lord, are my refuge and strength and "a very present help in trouble." Therefore I will not fear, "even though the earth be removed and though the mountains be carried to the midst of the sea" (Psalm 46:1-2).

Thank You, Lord, that no weapon formed against me will prosper (Isaiah 54:17). Thank You that You will not leave me in the hands of wicked people who would try to destroy me (Psalm 37:32-33). "Hide me under the shadow of Your wings, from the wicked who oppress me, from my deadly enemies who surround me" (Psalm 17:8). Protect me from the plans of evil people. Keep me from sudden danger. "Be merciful to me, O God, be merciful to me! For my soul trusts in You; and in the shadow of Your wings I will make my refuge" (Psalm 57:1). Thank You that "I will both lie down in peace, and sleep; for You alone, O LORD, make me dwell in safety" (Psalm 4:8). Thank You for Your promises of protection. I lay claim to them this day.

God's Promises to Me

Because you have made the LORD, who is my refuge,
even the Most High, your dwelling place,
no evil shall befall you, nor shall any
plague come near your dwelling.

Psalm 91:9-10

No weapon formed against you shall prosper.

Isaiah 54:17

When you pass through the waters, I will be with
you; and through the rivers, they shall not overflow
you. When you walk through the fire,
you shall not be burned, nor shall
the flame scorch you.

Isaiah 43:2

He shall cover you with His feathers, and under His
wings you shall take refuge; His truth shall be your
shield and buckler. You shall not be afraid of the
terror by night, nor of the arrow that flies by day, nor
of the pestilence that walks in darkness, nor of the
destruction that lays waste at noonday.
A thousand may fall at your side, and ten thousand
at your right hand; but it shall not come near you.

Psalm 91:4-7

He shall give His angels charge over you, to keep you
in all your ways.
PSALM 91:11

Chapter Eighteen

Lord, Give Me Wisdom to Make Right Decisions

As I was sitting out on the balcony of that same high-rise beachfront condominium I described in the previous chapter, I had a rare perspective of the water below. I could clearly see where there were very shallow places and where the ocean floor suddenly fell off, making the water very deep. I watched as people would swim a ways out and then find themselves in a place so shallow they were forced to stand up. The water at those places was barely knee level. It was fascinating to watch the swimmers walk around on the sandy plateau and then suddenly fall over the edge into deep water.

I realized that if I could have been connected to each of those swimmers by perhaps a waterproof cell phone or walkie-talkie, I could have told them when they were near the edge. But they had no connection with me. They didn't know to call. So I couldn't tell them what I saw from my perspective.

I think that's the way it is with God. He sees all because He is above all. If we were to connect with Him on a regular basis and say, "Lord, guide me so I won't fall," He could lead us away from the edge. But so often we don't make that connection with God. We don't call. We don't seek His guidance. We don't ask Him for wisdom. We don't consider His perspective. And too often we fall in over our heads because of it.

Lot, Abraham's nephew in the Bible, ended up being captured by the enemy because he chose to live in land that *he* thought was good (Genesis 13:10-11), but it was among wicked people (Genesis 13:13). He chose what *he* thought was best rather than what was *God's* best. How many times do people walk out from under God's umbrella of protection and away from *His* best, all because they have chosen what *they* think is best for their lives? They don't ask for *His* wisdom and *His* direction.

Haven't we all done that at one time or another? And just because we have walked with the Lord for some time doesn't make us immune to this problem. We may think we know God's will for a situation today because of what His will was the last time we asked. But what worked last year might not be the same thing He would direct us to do now. We always need to ask God for wisdom and guidance.

The things of God can only be discerned in the spirit. But the natural man doesn't get this. He can't. "The natural man does not receive the things of the Spirit of God, for they are foolishness to him; nor can he know them, because they are spiritually discerned" (1 Corinthians 2:14). Have you ever observed someone with no wisdom clearly doing the wrong thing or making a foolish decision? The consequences are crystal clear to you, but *they* don't see it at all. It's always easier to see a lack of wisdom in others than it is to see it in ourselves. That's why we must pray daily for wisdom.

Wisdom means having clear understanding and insight. It means knowing how to apply the truth in every situation. It's discerning what is right and wrong. It's having good judgment. It's being able to sense when you are getting too close to the edge. It's making the right choice or decision. And only God knows what that is. "When He, the Spirit of truth, has come, He will guide you into all truth; for He will not speak on His own authority, but whatever He hears He will speak; and He will tell you things to come" (John 16:13). We have no idea how many times simple wisdom has saved our lives or kept us out of harm's way or how many times it will do so in the future. That's why we can't live without it and need to ask God for it. We have to pray, "Lord give me wisdom in all I do. Help me to walk in wisdom every day."

Ten Good Ways to Walk in Wisdom

1. *Be in the Word of God.* "My son, if you receive my words, and treasure my commands within you, so that you incline your ear to wisdom, and apply your heart to understanding...then you will understand the fear of the LORD, and find the knowledge of God" (Proverbs 2:1-2,5).

2. *Pray for wisdom.* "If any of you lacks wisdom, let him ask of God, who gives to all liberally and without reproach, and it will be given to him" (James 1:5).

3. *Acknowledge the Lord in everything.* "In all your ways acknowledge Him, and He shall direct your paths" (Proverbs 3:6).

4. *Walk in reverence of God.* "The fear of the LORD is the beginning of wisdom" (Proverbs 9:10).

5. *Listen to wise people.* "Incline your ear and hear the words of the wise, and apply your heart to my knowledge" (Proverbs 22:17).

6. *Value wisdom above all*. "Get wisdom! Get understanding! Do not forget, nor turn away from the words of my mouth. Do not forsake her, and she will preserve you; love her, and she will keep you" (Proverbs 4:5-6).

7. *Walk in obedience*. He stores up sound wisdom for the upright; He is a shield to those who walk uprightly" (Proverbs 2:7).

8. *Be humble*. "When pride comes, then comes shame; but with the humble is wisdom" (Proverbs 11:2).

9. *Love your neighbor*. "He who is devoid of wisdom despises his neighbor, but a man of understanding holds his peace" (Proverbs 11:12).

10. *Seek the wisdom of God, not the wisdom of the world*. "But of Him you are in Christ Jesus, who became for us wisdom from God—and righteousness and sanctification and redemption" (1 Corinthians 1:30). "Has not God made foolish the wisdom of this world? For since, in the wisdom of God, the world through wisdom did not know God, it pleased God through the foolishness of the message preached to save those who believe" (1 Corinthians 1:20-21).

Ten Good Reasons to Ask for Wisdom

1. *To enjoy longevity, wealth, and honor*. "Length of days is in her right hand, in her left hand riches and honor" (Proverbs 3:16).

2. *To have a good life*. "Her ways are ways of pleasantness, and all her paths are peace" (Proverbs 3:17).

3. *To enjoy vitality and happiness*. "She is a tree of life to those who take hold of her, and happy are all who retain her" (Proverbs 3:18).

4. *To secure protection*. "Then you will walk safely in your way, and your foot will not stumble" (Proverbs 3:23).

5. *To experience refreshing rest*. "When you lie down, you will not be afraid; yes, you will lie down and your sleep will be sweet" (Proverbs 3:24).

6. *To gain confidence*. "For the LORD will be your confidence, and will keep your foot from being caught" (Proverbs 3:26).

7. *To know security*. "Do not forsake her, and she will preserve you; love her, and she will keep you...when you walk, your steps will not be hindered, and when you run, you will not stumble" (Proverbs 4:6,12).

8. *To be promoted*. "Exalt her, and she will promote you; she will bring you honor, when you embrace her" (Proverbs 4:8).

9. *To be protected*. "When wisdom enters your heart, and knowledge is pleasant to your soul, discretion will preserve you; understanding will keep you, to deliver you from the way of evil, from the man who speaks perverse things" (Proverbs 2:10-12).

10. *To gain understanding*. "A wise man will hear and increase learning, and a man of understanding will attain wise counsel" (Proverbs 1:5).

Seek the Counsel of God

It's important to always seek out God's counsel before you seek anyone else's. I don't mean that you can't take advice from your unbelieving doctor or lawyer. I'm saying that *before* you go to them, ask God *who* you are to go to and then ask Him to give that person wisdom and knowledge to impart to you. Ask God to show you if you are receiving any advice or guidance from a source that is not of the Lord. Ask Him to lead you away from any ungodly counsel and onto the path of the righteous and wise.

Just out of curiosity, I went down to the beach and out in the water to one of those shallow plateaus I had been observing. I walked around on top of it to see exactly how much of the depth of the water could be determined from that close perspective. Because I had the advantage of knowing there was a steep drop-off on one side, I confidently walked toward the edge. Suddenly the whole edge collapsed and I fell in just as I'd seen other swimmers do. With my pride dripping wet, I made my way back to shore. I realized that even when you *think* you know something, you still can't get too cocky. We will always need to ask God for His wisdom and counsel about *everything,* because He is the only one who knows the *whole* truth.

My Prayer to God

Lord, I pray You would give me Your wisdom and understanding in all things. I know wisdom is better than gold and understanding better than silver (Proverbs 16:16), so make me rich in wisdom and wealthy in understanding. Thank You that You give "wisdom to the wise and knowledge to those who have understanding" (Daniel 2:21). Increase my wisdom and knowledge so I can see Your truth in every situation. Give me discernment for each decision I must make.

Lord, help me to always seek godly counsel and not look to the world and ungodly people for answers. Thank You, Lord, that You will give me the counsel and instruction I need, even as I sleep. Thank You that "You will show me the path of life" (Psalm 16:7 11).

I delight in Your law and in Your Word. Help me to mediate on it day and night, to ponder it, to speak it, to memorize it, to get it into my soul and my heart. Lord, I know that whoever "trusts in his own heart is a fool, but whoever walks wisely will be delivered" (Proverbs 28:26). I don't want to trust my own heart. I want to trust Your Word and Your instruction so that I will walk wisely and never do ignorant or stupid things. Make me to be a wise person.

You said in Your Word that You store up sound wisdom for the upright (Proverbs 2:7). Help me to walk uprightly, righteously, and obediently to Your commands. May I never be wise in my own eyes, but may I always fear You. Keep me far from evil so that I can claim the health and strength Your Word promises (Proverbs 3:7-8). Give me the wisdom, knowledge, understanding, direction, and discernment I need to keep me away from the plans of evil so that I will walk safely and not stumble (Proverbs 2:10-13). Lord, I know that in You "are hidden all the treasures of wisdom and knowledge" (Colossians 2:3). Help me to discover those treasures.

God's Promises to Me

The fear of the LORD is the beginning of wisdom, and
the knowledge of the Holy One is understanding.
For by me your days will be multiplied, and
years of life will be added to you.
PROVERBS 9:10-11

The mouth of the righteous speaks wisdom,
and his tongue talks of justice.
The law of his God is in his heart;
none of his steps shall slide.
PSALM 37:30-31

Through wisdom a house is built, and by
understanding it is established; by knowledge the
rooms are filled with all precious and pleasant riches.
PROVERBS 24:3-4

Call to Me, and I will answer you, and show
you great and mighty things,
which you do not know.
JEREMIAH 33:3

If you cry out for discernment, and lift up your voice
for understanding, if you seek her as silver,
and search for her as for hidden treasures; then you
will understand the fear of the LORD, and find the
knowledge of God. For the LORD gives wisdom; from
His mouth come knowledge and understanding.
PROVERBS 2:3-6

Chapter Nineteen

Lord, Deliver Me from Every Evil Work

I know God as my Deliverer. He has set me free from many things, including alcohol, drugs, fear, depression, anxiety, and unforgiveness, to mention just a few. I have seen the Lord set me free in an instant, and I have also been through a process of deliverance that took years. Sometimes I had to fast and pray to get free, sometimes it took other strong believers praying for me, and sometimes it happened just by being in the Lord's presence. Regardless of *how* it happened, what matters most is that it *did.*

We all need deliverance at one time or another. That's because no matter how spiritual we are, we're still made of flesh. And no matter how perfectly we live, we still have an enemy who is trying to erect strongholds of evil in our lives. God wants us free from everything that binds, holds, or separates us from Him.

Jesus taught us to pray, "Deliver us from the evil one" (Matthew 6:13). He would not have instructed us in that manner if we didn't need to do it. But so often we don't pray that way, acting as if He never said it at all. So often we live our lives as if we don't realize Jesus paid an enormous price so we could be free. Jesus "gave Himself for our sins, that He might deliver us from this present evil age, according to the will of our God and Father" (Galatians 1:4). He wants to *continue* to set us free in the future.

God Wants You Free

Do you ever have trouble with finances to the point where it seems you will never get ahead? Are you constantly sick with one thing after another or with one reccurring illness that never gets diagnosed or cured? Do you feel that the things you do are never acknowledged as having worth? Are you hopelessly drawn to things that are not good for you, such as alcohol, food, drugs, ungodly relationships, or gambling? Are you drawn toward immorality? Do you find it impossible to rise above your resentment toward someone no matter how hard you try? Do you have continual strife in an important relationship?

Do you always feel distant from God no matter what you do? Does it seem as though your prayers are never being heard or answered? Do you feel discouraged and sad more than you feel the joy of the Lord? Do you find yourself coming back time and again to the same old problem, the same old habits of action and thought, the same old unhealthy situation? Do you always feel bad about yourself? If you said yes to any of these questions, I have good news for you. God wants to set you free. He wants you to remember that He is the Deliverer (Romans 11:26) and He promises to "deliver those who are drawn toward death" (Proverbs 24:11).

Do you realize that any one of these inclinations or symptoms could be the enemy's weapon formed against you? So often we go along with the devil's plans for our lives, not knowing we don't have to put up with it. We think it's just fate or bad luck when it's really the enemy. But Jesus came to set us free from all the things that bind us. He came to lift us above the enemy who wants to destroy us. God hears the groaning of those who are held captive (Psalm 102:19-20). If you cry out to Him, He will set you free. And "if the Son makes you free, you shall be free indeed" (John 8:36). No matter how strong the thing is you're struggling with, God's power to deliver you is stronger.

God wants you free not only because He loves you and has compassion upon you, but because He wants you to be able to "serve Him without fear, in holiness and righteousness before Him," all the days of your life (Luke 1:74-75). Of course, we are responsible to *walk away* from evil. The Bible says, "The highway of the upright is to depart from evil; he who keeps his way preserves his soul" (Proverbs 16:17). Sometimes *we* are responsible for the things that happen in our lives. But sometimes there are plans of the enemy erected against us that we must be delivered from.

How to Find Freedom

Deliverance is found by praying for it yourself (Psalm 72:12), by having someone else who is a strong believer pray with you for it (Psalm 34:17), by reading the truth of God's Word with great understanding and clarity (John 8:32), or by spending time in the Lord's presence. The most effective and powerful way to spend time in the Lord's presence is in praise and worship. Every time you worship God, something happens in the spirit realm to break the power of evil. That's because He inhabits your praises, and this means you are in His presence. "Now the Lord is the Spirit; and where the Spirit of the Lord is, there is liberty" (2 Corinthians 3:17).

The Bible says, "The angel of the LORD encamps all around those who fear Him, and delivers them" (Psalm 34:7). Whenever the enemy tries to tell you that you will never get free, drown him out with praise. Thank God that He is the Deliverer and you are being delivered even as you praise Him. And once you have been set free, tell others about it. "Let the redeemed of the LORD say so, whom He has redeemed from the hand of the enemy" (Psalm 107:2).

If you ever seem to be sliding back into the very thing you've already been set free of, don't even waste time getting discouraged. Often what seems like the same old thing coming back again may be a new layer surfacing that needs to come off. You're not going backwards—you are going deeper. Those deep layers of bondage can hurt far worse than the earlier ones. Trust that your times are in His hands, and He will deliver you in His timing (Psalm 31:14-15).

Remember that deliverance comes from the Lord, and it is an ongoing process. It is God who has "delivered us from so great a death, and does deliver us; in whom we trust that He will still deliver us" (2 Corinthians 1:10). God does a complete work, and He will see it through to the end. So don't give up because it's taking longer than you hoped. Be confident that "He who has begun a good work in you will complete it until the day of Jesus Christ" (Philippians 1:6).

He will not rest until your righteousness goes forth as brightness and your salvation as a lamp that burns (Isaiah 62:1). Deliverance won't change you into someone else. It will release you to be who you really are—an intelligent, secure, loving, talented, kindhearted, witty, attractive, wonderful woman of God.

My Prayer to God

Lord, thank You that You have promised to "deliver me from every evil work and preserve me" for Your heavenly kingdom (2 Timothy 4:18). I know that "we do not wrestle against flesh and blood, but against principalities, against powers, against the rulers of the darkness of this age, against spiritual hosts of wickedness in the heavenly places" (Ephesians 6:12). Thank You that You have put all these enemies under Your feet (Ephesians 1:22), and "there is nothing covered that will not be revealed, and hidden that will not be known" (Matthew 10:26).

Lord, I know that I can't see all the ways the enemy wants to erect strongholds in my life. I depend on You to reveal them to me. Thank You that You came to "proclaim liberty to the captives and recovery of sight to the blind, to set at liberty those who are oppressed" (Luke 4:18). Without You I am held captive by my desires, I am blind to the truth, and I am oppressed. But with You comes freedom from all that. "My times are in Your hand; deliver me from the hand of my enemies, and from those who persecute me" (Psalm 31:15).

I know that my deliverance comes from You. Thank You that You "drew me out of many waters" and "delivered me from my strong enemy" (Psalm 18:16-17). Help me to stand fast in the liberty by which Christ has made me free, and help me not to become tangled in any yoke of bondage (Galatians 5:1).

I call upon You, Lord, and ask that You would deliver me from anything that binds me or separates me from You. I specifically ask to be delivered from (name a specific area where you want to be set free). Where I have opened the door for the enemy with my own desires, I repent of that. Where I am walking in disobedience, show me so I can turn and live in obedience to Your ways. Give me wisdom to walk the right way and strength to rise above the things that would pull me down (Proverbs 28:26).

I know that though I walk in the flesh, I do not war according to the flesh because "the weapons of our warfare are not carnal but mighty in God for pulling down strongholds" (2 Corinthians 10:3-4). In Jesus' name, I pray that every stronghold erected around me by the enemy will be brought down to nothing. Make darkness light before me and the crooked places straight (Isaiah 42:16). I know that You who have begun a good work in me will complete it (Philippians 1:6). Give me patience to not give up and the strength to stand strong in Your Word.

God's Promises to Me

The righteous cry out, and the LORD hears, and delivers them out of all their troubles.

Psalm 34:17

Call upon Me in the day of trouble; I will deliver you, and you shall glorify Me.

Psalm 50:15

I will give you the keys of the kingdom of heaven, and whatever you bind on earth will be bound in heaven, and whatever you loose on earth will be loosed in heaven.
MATTHEW 16:19

He who trusts in his own heart is a fool, but whoever walks wisely will be delivered.
PROVERBS 28:26

Because he has set his love upon Me, therefore I will deliver him; I will set him on high, because he has known My name.
PSALM 91:14

Chapter Twenty

Lord, Set Me Free from Negative Emotions

I used to think that living with anxiety, depression, fear, and hopelessness was a way of life. *This is just the way I am,* I thought. But when I came to know the Lord and started living God's way, I began to see that *all* things are possible to anyone who believes and obeys God. It's even possible to live without negative emotions. God will take them off of us like a thick wet blanket if we ask Him to. But we have to pray.

Have you ever felt as though God has forsaken you? Well, if you have, you're not alone. In fact, you are in very good company. Not only do millions of other people feel that way right now, but Jesus felt that way at one time too. At the lowest point in His life, Jesus said, "My God, my God, why have You forsaken Me?" (Matthew 27:46). We all have difficult times. Times when we feel all alone and abandoned. But the truth is we aren't. God is with us to help us when we call upon Him. In the midst of these times, we don't have to be controlled by our negative emotions. We can resist them by praying and knowing the truth of what God's Word says about them.

Seven Good Ways to Get Free of Negative Emotions

1. *Refuse to be anxious*. No matter what problems we have in our life, Jesus has overcome them. "In the world you will have tribulation; but be of good cheer, I have overcome the world" (John 16:33). We can find freedom from anxiety just by spending time with Him. "In the multitude of my anxieties within me, Your comforts delight my soul" (Psalm 94:19).

When you are anxious, it means you aren't trusting God to take care of you. But He will prove His faithfulness if you run to Him. "Do not seek what you should eat or what you should drink, nor have an anxious mind. For all these things the nations of the world seek after, and your Father knows that you need these things. But seek the kingdom of God, and all these things shall be added to you" (Luke 12:29-31). God says we don't need to be anxious about *anything*; we just need to pray about *everything*.

2. *Refuse to be ruled by anger*. When we frequently give place to anger it shuts off all God has for us the way pressure on a hose shuts off the water flow. I've seen it happen countless times with people. Just when God is moving in their lives in a powerful way, they give in to anger and completely shut Him off. When we give anger a home in our souls, we open the door to sin and the devil. " 'Be angry, and do not sin': do not let the sun go down on your wrath, nor give place to the devil" (Ephesians 4:26-27).

An angry person upsets everyone around them, and they make serious mistakes as a result. "An angry man stirs up strife, and a furious man abounds in transgression" (Proverbs 29:22). How many angry men abuse their wives, or even kill them, and destroy their lives forever because of it? How many angry women destroy their relationships and their families and sacrifice the destiny God has for them?

Only foolish people are quick to get angry. People with wisdom don't want to pay the price. "Do not hasten in your spirit to be angry, for anger rests in the bosom of fools" (Ecclesiastes 7:9). Ask God to keep you free from anger so you can remain in the flow of all God has for you.

3. *Refuse to be dissatisfied.* It's easy to focus on the negative and look for everything that's wrong with your life. But when we have constant unrest because we are never at peace, it not only makes *us* miserable—it makes everyone around us miserable too. There is nothing wrong with wanting things to be different when they need to be, but when that attitude becomes a way of life, we sacrifice our peace. Whenever you feel discouraged by your circumstances, remember that the apostle Paul said "I have learned in whatever state I am, to be content: I know how to be abased, and I know how to abound. Everywhere and in all things I have learned both to be full and to be hungry, both to abound and to suffer need. I can do all things through Christ who strengthens me" (Philippians 4:11-13).

God promises you rest. "There remains therefore a rest for the people of God" (Hebrews 4:9). It's possible to find contentment, rest, peace, and joy in any situation. Tell God you are making that your goal and you need Him to help you.

4. *Refuse to be envious.* When you set your eyes on someone else and what *they* have instead of on the Lord and what *He* has, a covetous spirit is about to make your life miserable. "For where envy and self-seeking exist, confusion and every evil thing are there. But the wisdom that is from above is first pure, then peaceable, gentle, willing to yield, full of mercy and good fruits, without partiality and without hypocrisy" (James 3:16-17). Don't allow yourself to entertain thoughts such as, "If only I had *her* hair...*her* face...*her* body...*her* clothes...*her* talent...*her* gifts...*her* husband...*her*

kids...*her* wealth...*her* luck...*her* blessings." Turn your thoughts toward Jesus instead. Think about *His* beauty, *His* wealth, *His* talents, *His* nature, *His* provision, *His* help, and *His* power. Thank Him for the rich inheritance you have in Him, and tell Him you can't wait to experience it all.

Covetousness started when Cain wanted what Abel had, and he killed him for it. But he suffered the rest of his life as a result. "Where there are envy, strife, and divisions among you, are you not carnal and behaving like mere men?" (1 Corinthians 3:3). We don't want to suffer for the rest of our lives because of covetousness. The price we pay for envy is way too high. "A sound heart is life to the body, but envy is rottenness to the bones" (Proverbs 14:30). Ask for God's love to be manifested in you and through you at all times. "Love suffers long and is kind; love does not envy" (1 Corinthians 13:4).

5. *Refuse to be depressed.* Of all the negative emotions, I believe depression is the one we most readily accept as part of our lives. So many of us live with depression and accept it without even realizing it. It feels natural to us because it is so familiar. But God doesn't want us to accept this as a way of life.

Many people of the Bible understood what depression feels like. "I am weary with my groaning; all night I make my bed swim; I drench my couch with my tears. My eye wastes away because of grief; it grows old because of all my enemies" (Psalm 6:6-7). "Reproach has broken my heart, and I am full of heaviness; I looked for someone to take pity, but there was none; and for comforters, but I found none" (Psalm 69:20). "My soul melts from heaviness; strengthen me according to Your word" (Psalm 119:28). Does any of this sound familiar? The good news is that God doesn't want us to live with these feelings. He wants us to have the joy of the Lord rise in us and chase away spirits of heaviness. "Depart from me, all you workers of iniquity; for the LORD has heard the voice of my weeping. The LORD has heard my supplication; the LORD will receive my prayer" (Psalm 6:8-9). God wants us to cry out to Him so He can lift us out of depression.

6. *Refuse to be bitter*. Bitterness burns away your body and soul the way acid eats skin. When a root of bitterness takes hold of your life, it consumes you and cuts off the blessings of God. "For I see that you are poisoned by bitterness and bound by iniquity" (Acts 8:23). When we constantly have thoughts such as, "How long shall I take counsel in my soul, having sorrow in my heart daily? How long will my enemy be exalted over me?" (Psalm 13:2), then we have bitterness growing in us like a cancer. But we can identify those thoughts and refuse to give place to them. We can ask God to help us resist them. "Looking diligently lest anyone fall short of the grace of God; lest any root of bitterness springing up cause trouble, and by this many become defiled" (Hebrews 12:15).

Pray for God to set you free from any bitterness. Ask Him to give you a spirit of thankfulness, praise, and worship. Ask the Holy Spirit to crowd out anything in your heart that is not of Him.

7. *Refuse to be hopeless*. Hopelessness is a slow killer that will eventually affect the health of your body and soul. But when you deliberately choose to put your hope in the Lord, He will meet all your needs and take all hopelessness away. Just as we can choose what attitude we will have every day, we can choose to put our hope in God. We can guard our soul. "Thorns and snares are in the way of the perverse; He who guards his soul will be far from them" (Proverbs 22:5). Hopelessness is death to our souls. Refuse to live with it. No

matter how bad things appear to get in your life, you *always* have hope in the Lord. Ask God to give you hope for your future and an attitude of gratefulness every day of your life.

Negative emotions reveal doubt. If we thoroughly trust God, what do we have to be anxious about? Why would we be angry, dissatisfied, envious, depressed, bitter, or hopeless? Yet we all are susceptible to experiencing these kinds of emotions at some time in our life. So don't feel bad about having them, but don't live with them either. Refuse to allow the ugliness of negative emotions to mar the beauty of the life God has for you.

My Prayer to God

Lord, help me to live in Your joy and peace. Give me strength and understanding to resist anxiety, anger, unrest, envy, depression, bitterness, hopelessness, loneliness, fear, and guilt. Rescue me when "my spirit is overwhelmed within me; my heart within me is distressed" (Psalm 143:4). I refuse to let my life be brought down by negative emotions such as these. I know You have a better quality of life for me than that. When I am tempted to give in to them, show me Your truth.

You have said in Your Word that by our patience we can possess our souls (Luke 21:19). Give me patience so that I can do that. Help me to keep my "heart with all diligence," for I know that "out of it spring the issues of life" (Proverbs 4:23). Help me to not be insecure and self-focused so that I miss opportunities to focus on You and extend Your love. May I be sensitive to the needs, trials, and weaknesses of others and not oversensitive to myself.

What You accomplished on the cross is my source of greatest joy. Help me to concentrate on that.

"The enemy has persecuted my soul; he has crushed my life to the ground; he has made me dwell in darkness, like those who have long been dead. Therefore my spirit is overwhelmed within me; my heart within me is distressed. I remember the days of old; I meditate on all Your works; I muse on the work of Your hands. I spread out my hands to You; my soul longs for You like a thirsty land. Answer me speedily, O LORD; my spirit fails! Do not hide Your face from me, lest I be like those who go down into the pit. Cause me to hear Your lovingkindness in the morning, for in You do I trust; cause me to know the way in which I should walk, for I lift up my soul to You" (Psalm 143:3-8). Thank You, Lord, that in my distress I can call on You. And when I cry out to You, Lord, You hear my voice and answer (Psalm 18:6). May the joy of knowing You fill my heart with happiness and peace.

GOD'S *PROMISES* TO ME

Be anxious for nothing, but in everything by prayer and supplication, with thanksgiving, let your requests be made known to God; and the peace of God, which surpasses all understanding, will guard your hearts and minds through Christ Jesus.

PHILIPPIANS 4:6-7

Then they cried out to the LORD in their trouble, and He saved them out of their distresses. He brought them out of darkness and the shadow of death, and broke their chains in pieces.

PSALM 107:13-14

Come to Me, all you who labor and are heavy laden, and I will give you rest. Take My yoke upon you and learn from Me, for I am gentle and lowly in heart, and you will find rest for your souls. For My yoke is easy and My burden is light.

MATTHEW 11:28-30

The righteous cry out, and the LORD hears, and delivers them out of all their troubles. The LORD is near to those who have a broken heart, and saves such as have a contrite spirit.

PSALM 34:17-18

Those who wait on the LORD shall renew their strength; they shall mount up with wings like eagles, they shall run and not be weary, they shall walk and not faint.

ISAIAH 40:31

Chapter Twenty-One

Lord, Comfort Me in Times of Trouble

Every time I take off in an airplane on a gray, dreary, rainy day, I'm always amazed at how we can fly right up through the dark wet clouds, so thick that we can't see one thing out the window, and then suddenly rise above it all and have the ability to see for miles. Up there the sky is sunny, clear, and blue. I keep forgetting that no matter how bad the weather gets, it's possible to rise above the storm to a place where everything is fine.

Our spiritual and emotional lives are much the same. When the dark clouds of trial, struggle, grief, or suffering roll in and settle on us so thick that we can barely see ahead of us, it's easy to forget there is a place of calm, light, clarity, and peace we can rise to. If we take God's hand in those difficult times, He will lift us up above our circumstances to the place of comfort, warmth, and safety He has for us.

One of my favorite names for the Holy Spirit is the Comforter (John 14:26 ASV). Just as we don't have to beg the sun for light, we don't have to beg the Holy Spirit for comfort either. He *is* comfort. We simply have to separate ourselves from anything that separates us from Him. We have to pray that when we go through difficult times, He will give us a greater sense of His comfort in it.

Tough times happen to everyone at one time or another. Pain and loss are a part of life. There are many different reasons why these things occur, but God is always there to bring good out of it when we invite Him to. If we understand the different possibilities for our suffering, it will help us overcome our pain and see our faith grow in the midst of it.

Four Good Reasons for Difficult Times

1. *Sometimes difficult things happen to us so that the glory and power of God can be revealed in and through us.* When Jesus passed by a man who was born blind, His disciples asked Him if the man's blindness was because he had sinned or because his parents had sinned. Jesus replied, "Neither this man nor his parents sinned, but that the works of God should be revealed in him" (John 9:3). We may not be able to understand why certain things are happening at the time, and we may never know why we have to go through them until we go to be with the Lord, but when we turn to God in the midst of difficult situations, God's glory will be seen in them and on you.

2. *God uses difficult times to purify us.* The Bible says, "Since Christ suffered for us in the flesh, arm yourselves also with the same mind, for he who has suffered in the flesh has ceased from sin" (1 Peter 4:1). This means our suffering during difficult times will burn sin and selfishness out of our lives. God allows suffering to happen so that we will learn to live for Him and not for ourselves. So that we will pursue His will and not our own. It's not pleasant at the time, but God's desire is "that we may be partakers of His holiness" (Hebrews 12:10). He wants us to let go of the things we lust after and cling to what is most important in life—Him.

3. *Sometimes our misery is caused by God disciplining us.* "No chastening seems to be joyful for the present, but painful; nevertheless, afterward it yields the peaceable fruit of righteousness to those who have been trained by it" (Hebrews 12:11). The fruit that this godly disciplining and pruning produces in us is worth the trouble we have to go through to get it, and we have to be careful not to resist it or hate it. "Do not despise the chastening of the LORD, nor be discouraged when you are rebuked by Him; for whom the LORD loves He chastens, and scourges every son whom He receives" (Hebrews 12:5-6).

4. *Sometimes we are caught in the midst of the enemy's work.* It's the enemy's delight to make you miserable and try to destroy your life. Often the reason for the anguish, sorrow, sadness, grief, or pain you feel is entirely his doing and no fault of your own or anyone else's. Your comfort is in knowing that as you praise God in the midst of it, He will defeat the enemy and bring good out of it that you can't even fathom. He wants you to walk with Him in faith as He leads you through it, and He will teach you to trust Him in the midst of it.

None of us wants to hear about how good pain and suffering are for us. When we're in the midst of trouble, tragedy, loss, devastation, or disappointment, we hurt terribly and find it impossible to think beyond the pain. But the Holy Spirit is there to help us. In other translations of the Bible, He is called the Helper. Jesus said, "I will pray the Father, and He will give you another Helper, that He may abide with you forever—the Spirit of truth" (John 14:16-17). When we turn to the Holy Spirit for help and comfort, He will not only give us aid, but He will give us a richer portion of His presence than we have ever had before. We will be blessed when we mourn, because it will be the Comforter who comforts us (Matthew 5:4).

When my friend died of breast cancer a number of years ago, I was devastated with grief. We had been best friends since high school, and I didn't know how I could survive the loss. The day after the funeral was the worst pain of all. Reality set in and I couldn't stop crying. Plus, along with my six- and ten-year-old children, I now had her eight-year-old son to care for too. I asked God to lift me out of my grief so I could function well enough to help him cope with his loss. God answered that prayer every day as I turned to Him for strength and comfort.

Every time you rise above the pain in your life and find the goodness, clarity, peace, and light of the Lord there, your faith will increase. God will meet you in the midst of your pain and not only perfect you, but increase your compassion for the sufferings of others. As you continue to live in the presence of the Lord, His glory will be revealed in you.

My Prayer to God

Lord, help me to remember that no matter how dark my situation may become, You are the light of my life and can never be put out. No matter what dark clouds settle on my life, You will lift me above the storm and into the comfort of Your presence. Only You can take whatever loss I experience and fill that empty place with good. Only You can take the burden of my grief and pain and dry my tears. "Hear me when I call, O God of my righteousness! You have relieved me in my distress; have mercy on me, and hear my prayer" (Psalm 4:1).

In times of grief, suffering, or trial, I pray for an added sense of Your presence. I want to grow stronger in these times and not weaker. I want to increase in faith and not be overcome with doubt. I want to have hope in the midst of it and not surrender to hopelessness. I want to stand strong in Your truth and not be swept away by my emotions.

Thank You that I do not have to be afraid of bad news because my heart is steadfast, trusting in You (Psalm 112:7). Thank You that "You have delivered my soul from death, my eyes from tears, and my feet from falling" (Psalm 116:8). Thank You that I walk before You with hope in my heart and life in my body. Thank You that "I shall not die, but live, and declare the works of the LORD" (Psalm 118:17). Even when "my soul melts from heaviness," I pray that You would "strengthen me according to Your word" (Psalm 119:28).

Help me to remember to give thanks to You in all things, knowing that You reign in the midst of them. Remind me that You have redeemed me and I am Yours and nothing is more important than that. I know when I pass through the waters You will be with me and the river will not overflow me. When I walk through the fire I will not be burned, nor will the flame touch me (Isaiah 43:1-2). That's because You are a good God and have sent Your Holy Spirit to comfort and help me. I pray that You, O God of hope, will fill me with all joy and peace and faith so that I will "abound in hope by the power of the Holy Spirit" (Romans 15:13). Thank You that You have sent Your Holy Spirit to be my Comforter and Helper. Remind me of that in the midst of difficult times.

God's Promises to Me

Beloved, do not think it strange concerning the fiery trial which is to try you, as though some strange thing happened to you; but rejoice to the extent that you partake of Christ's sufferings, that when His glory is revealed, you may also be glad with exceeding joy.

1 Peter 4:12-13

May the God of all grace, who called us to His eternal glory by Christ Jesus, after you have suffered a while, perfect, establish, strengthen, and settle you.

1 Peter 5:10

Wait on the LORD; be of good courage, and He shall strengthen your heart; wait, I say, on the LORD!

Psalm 27:14

Blessed are the poor in spirit, for theirs
is the kingdom of heaven.
Blessed are those who mourn,
for they shall be comforted.

Matthew 5:3-4

The LORD shall preserve your going out and
your coming in from this time forth,
and even forevermore.

Psalm 121:8

CHAPTER TWENTY-TWO

Lord, Enable Me to Resist the Temptation to Sin

Why would a young man with everything going for him want to risk losing it all? One particular man I know of had good looks, musical talent, courage, wealth, prominence, authority, a wife, and God's favor. In addition to all this, he had single-handedly defeated one of the worst enemy threats to his nation's military. Yet he fell into temptation and succumbed to it with sin on top of sin.

King David obviously had too much time on his hands *and* he wasn't where he was supposed to be. He was out on the roof of his palace watching the woman next door take a bath instead of going to war with his men the way other kings did. His biggest mistake was not that he fell into temptation, for that can happen to anyone, but that he didn't turn away from it and run to God in repentance immediately. He stayed and stared. He thought and schemed. He let his lust rule him instead of his God. As a result, he became a murderer and an adulterer and ended up paying for it for the rest of his life—even to the point of witnessing the death of his own son.

Temptation happened to Jesus, too. But He did the right thing and David did not. David went with the lust of his flesh and Jesus didn't. Jesus stood strong in the Word of God and David forgot about it.

I have lived long enough, and I'm sure you have too, to have seen far too many people—men and women both—sacrifice their lives by giving in to temptation. There are many kinds of temptation, just as there are many kinds of sin. The one that seems to trip people up most often is sexual temptation. I have seen talented people succumb to sexual temptation and forfeit the promising life God had for them. They fell like meteors and burned themselves out when they could have been a shining star today. Even though they have been redeemed and restored, I have never seen them regain the anointing and glory of God that was once upon them.

When people fall into adultery, the life they *would* have had is forever sacrificed. Of course, when they repent they can receive forgiveness and be restored, but they have lost what *would* have been had this sin never happened. David was forgiven and restored, but he lost the thing he loved most—his son—and his reign was marred from that point on with one disaster after another, including the destruction of many of his beloved family members. God still loved him, but his sin still had consequences. People don't realize how much they lose when they give in to sexual temptation. Their light never shines as brightly as it would have if they had not given in to the lust of their flesh.

From the volumes of mail I receive I know that improper attraction to a person of the opposite sex is the biggest temptation for many men and women. Often it is not acted upon, but it is still entertained in the mind. And sins of the mind have serious consequences too. Sexual sin begins with thoughts such as, "This is the person of my dreams, never mind that he (she) is married and I am married." "This must be right or I wouldn't feel so good doing it." "I deserve to have what I want." "No one will ever know." "This must be fate."

Don't let the devil rob you of all God has for you by tempting you with impure thoughts. It's okay to appreciate a man's talents, godliness, brilliance, or appearance, but unless you are married to him, remember that he is your brother in the Lord. If you ever find yourself with any kind of unholy attraction, confess it immediately before God and ask Him to set you free from it. Then tell Satan that you recognize his plan to destroy you and separate you from all God has for you, and you are not going to allow him to do it. Fast and pray if you have to in order to break down that stronghold. Don't let up until it's gone. "Watch and pray, lest you enter into temptation. The spirit indeed is willing, but the flesh is weak" (Matthew 26:41). The more you have been given, the more you will be approached by the enemy who will try to take it away from you. Be ready for him with a full knowledge of the Word of God.

Six Good Things to Remember About Temptation

1. *Who:* Temptation can happen to anyone. No matter how spiritual and solid you think you are, you can fall into temptation. The people I have seen who fell the hardest were those who were prideful about what good Christians they were. They bragged about their spiritual strength and godliness, and yet they fell the hardest and without repentance. We can't let spiritual pride be our downfall.

2. *What:* You can be tempted by anything. The most common temptation today is sexual because the opportunity for it is everywhere. But there are other kinds of lust as

well. Money tempts us. Power tempts us. Desire tempts us. "Each one is tempted when he is drawn away by his own desires and enticed. Then, when desire has conceived, it gives birth to sin; and sin, when it is full-grown, brings forth death. Do not be deceived, my beloved brethren" (James 1:14-16). The enemy will tempt you in the way you are most susceptible. Whatever your flesh lusts after, ask God to give you the strength to resist it. Guard your vulnerable areas with prayer.

3. *When:* Temptation can happen any time and often when you least expect it and are most susceptible. When it does happen, the danger is in thinking you can handle it alone. It's best to take it to God and confess it immediately, and then find someone trustworthy to pray with you about it. Don't think it will just pass. The risk is too great. Treat it as a serious threat no matter when it happens.

4. *Where:* Temptation can happen anywhere. In church, at work, at home, on a bus or plane. It will happen in the place you least expect it. Wherever it is, separate yourself from it immediately. If chocolate tempts you, don't hang out in the candy store. The smell of it will drive you crazy and weaken your resistance. If a certain man tempts you, don't be around him. Or if you must, don't be alone with him. Separate yourself from the temptation and ask God to kill that lust in you.

5. *Why:* The reason the enemy tempts you is because he knows of the great things God wants to do in your life, and he thinks you are dumb enough to give it all up for a few moments of pleasure. He knows that not only do *you* stand to lose from it, but other people will be hurt by your sin as well. So he has the potential for multiple victories. When you see his trap, tell him you are not going to allow him to destroy your life or anyone else's.

6. *How:* You have to remember that no matter how you are being tempted, it is a set-up by the enemy intended to bring you down. He will find your weakness, need, or insecurity and tempt you with whatever you are most easily tempted. This is the best reason to get rid of all insecurities and become whole people. It eliminates one of the ways the enemy has access to our lives.

The best time to pray about temptation is *before* you fall into it. After the lure presents itself, resisting temptation becomes much more difficult. The model prayer Jesus taught us to pray as a matter of course is a good place to start. "Do not lead us into temptation, but deliver us from the evil one" (Matthew 6:13). We can also do as Jesus did and rebuke the enemy with God's Word. We can "stand fast therefore in the liberty by which Christ has made us free, and do not be entangled again with a yoke of bondage" (Galatians 5:1). We can call on the name of the Lord "for in that He Himself has suffered, being tempted, He is able to aid those who are tempted" (Hebrews 2:18).

Don't ever think you are immune to temptation. The older you get, the more you are a target. Many people fail when they get older because they think they can get away with it. You don't want to be the kind of person who believes for a while and in time of temptation falls away (Luke 8:13). Jesus instructed His disciples to "rise and pray, lest you enter into temptation." You must do the same.

Jesus' temptation happened just before the greatest breakthrough in His life and ministry. It will happen before the greatest breakthrough in yours too. Be ready for it. And remember that no matter how great the temptation is you face, "He who is in you is greater than he who is in the world" (1 John 4:4). You have the power to overcome it.

My Prayer to God

Lord, help me to be strong in my mind and spirit so I don't fall into any traps of the enemy. Do not allow me to be led into temptation, but deliver me from the evil one and his plans for my downfall. The area I am most concerned about is (name any area where you might be tempted). In the name of Jesus, I break any hold temptation has on me. Keep me strong and able to resist anything that would tempt me away from all You have for me.

I pray I will have no secret thoughts where I entertain ungodly desires to do or say something I shouldn't. I pray that I will have no secret life where I do things I would be ashamed to have others see. I don't want to have fellowship with unfruitful works of darkness. Help me, instead, to expose them (Ephesians 5:11). Make straight paths for my feet (Hebrews 12:13). Don't allow the enemy to sneak up on my blind side and take me by surprise.

I know You are "not the author of confusion but of peace" (1 Corinthians 14:33). Help me not to fall into any confusion about this. Help me to hide Your Word in my heart so I will see clearly and not sin against You in any way (Psalm 119:11). By the power of Your Spirit in me, I will not allow sin to reign in me or draw me to obey its lusts (Romans 6:12).

Thank You, Lord, that You are near to all who call upon You, and You will fulfill the desire of those who fear You. Thank You that You hear my cries and will save me from any weakness that could lead me away from all You have for me (Psalm 145:18-19). Thank You that You know "how to deliver the godly out of temptations" (2 Peter 2:9). Thank You that You will deliver me out of all temptation and keep it far from me.

GOD'S *PROMISES TO* ME

Blessed is the man who endures temptation; for when he has been approved, he will receive the crown of life which the Lord has promised to those who love Him.

JAMES 1:12

No temptation has overtaken you except such as is common to man; but God is faithful, who will not allow you to be tempted beyond what you are able, but with the temptation will also make the way of escape, that you may be able to bear it.

1 CORINTHIANS 10:13

Let us lay aside every weight, and the sin which so easily ensnares us, and let us run with endurance the race that is set before us, looking unto Jesus, the author and finisher of our faith, who for the joy that was set before Him endured the cross, despising the shame, and has sat down at the right hand of the throne of God.

HEBREWS 12:1-2

My brethren, count it all joy when you fall into various trials, knowing that the testing of your faith produces patience. But let patience have its perfect work, that you may be perfect and complete, lacking nothing.

JAMES 1:2-4

Therefore let him who thinks he stands take heed lest he fall.

1 CORINTHIANS 10:12

Chapter Twenty-Three

Lord, Heal Me and Help Me Care for My Body

I almost died two years ago. I had been extremely sick in my abdominal area for months, and I was in and out of different emergency rooms and hospitals, seeing different doctors and specialists, but none of these people could find anything wrong with me. All the tests came back proving I was as healthy as I could possibly be. No one could figure out why I was so miserable.

In the middle of the most awful night I have ever experienced in my life, I felt something explode in my body so violently that I knew I would die if I didn't get help. My husband rushed me to the hospital at 3:30 in the morning because I didn't have time to wait for an ambulance. But then I laid in the emergency room for hours begging someone to help me and telling people I was going to die if somebody didn't do something soon. I was given all the same tests they had given me many times before, and still no one could find anything wrong with me.

My husband prayed for me continually, and when my sister, Susan, and my close friend, Roz, arrived at the hospital, they prayed for me too. They called other people to pray that someone would figure out what was wrong and do something. I couldn't pray anything for myself except, "Help me, Jesus."

At one point I said to God, "Is this my time to die?" But I did not sense God saying that it was. In fact, I felt Him say there were things He still had for me to do.

It wasn't until eight hours after I was brought in to the hospital that a specialist called a surgeon in who was brave enough to say, "I can't tell what's wrong with you by any of the tests, but I believe your appendix has ruptured. I am going to take you into surgery immediately, and if I'm wrong I'll find out what the problem is."

As it turned out, he was right. After the surgery the doctor said, "In another hour you would have gone into a toxic-shock coma, and I could not have saved your life." I knew God had answered our prayers for healing and this surgeon was an important part of that answer.

For the next two weeks, I was hooked up to tubes and a machine and endured pain that made childbirth seem pleasant. Even constant morphine couldn't take it all away. When the doctor came to check on me one morning, I asked him why this had happened.

"Did I do something wrong?" I asked. "Did I take too many vitamins? Did I take too few? Did I take the wrong ones? Did I not exercise enough? Or too much? I have always tried to take good care of myself. Could I have done something differently to avoid this?"

"You couldn't have done anything to prevent this," he replied. "It's probably genetic and runs in your family."

He was right again. There were many people in my family who had experienced this same problem, only at a much younger age than I. In fact, I thought nothing like this would happen to me because I had passed the age when it occurred in other family members. I realized that no matter how hard we try to do the right thing, we can't always prevent bad things from happening in our body. We should do the best we can to take care of ourselves, but we will still always need God to be our Healer.

Two Separate Issues

Healing and body care are two different things. When you ask God to heal you, this is something *He* does. Taking care of your body is something *you* do. Both are vitally important.

God knows we are a fallen race and can't do everything perfectly. That's why He sent Jesus to be our Healer. But He also calls us to be good stewards over everything He gives us, including our body. He wants us to live in balance and temperance and to take care not to abuse our body in any way. He wants us to glorify Him in the care of our bodies because we are the temple of His Holy Spirit.

Many of us tend to think, "Everything I have is the Lord's, except for my eating and exercise habits. Those are mine." Or we think, "My life is the Lord's, but my body belongs to me, and I can do with it whatever feels good." But when we are the Lord's, our body has to be surrendered to Him just like everything else. Caring for our body is not something we can do successfully independent of God.

The motivation for what we do in the area of body care is very important. It will effect how successful we are. If we eat right and exercise merely to look great in our clothes, it won't be enough to sustain us as we get older. But if we eat right and engage in proper exercise for the purpose of being a more vital, healthy, energetic, and useful servant of the Lord, this has eternal consequences and you are more likely to stick with it.

I've actually heard people say, "I don't worry about taking care of my body because the Lord can just heal me when I get sick." This kind of presumptuous thinking is dangerous and can get us into trouble. Satan's plan for our lives is to do the very thing that will hurt us the most. We help him along by that kind of attitude. We sabotage our lives by not doing what's best for bodies and our health. Ask God to help you resist what is bad for you and to be disciplined enough to do what's right. God loves and values you. He created you. You are where His Holy Spirit dwells. He wants you to love and value yourself enough to take good care of your body.

In Touch with the Healer

In spite of all our best efforts, however, we can still get sick. We can do everything we know to do and still become seriously ill. That's because through no fault of our own we inherit predispositions or weaknesses from our ancestors. We can be exposed to things we aren't even aware of at the time that cause horrific diseases. We can have accidents. God knew all this, and so He sent Jesus as our Healer. His healing touch is God's mercy to us.

In the Bible, people who simply *touched* Jesus were healed. "Wherever He entered, into villages, cities, or in the country, they laid the sick in the marketplaces, and begged Him that they might just touch the hem of His garment. And as many as touched Him were made well" (Mark 6:56). We, too, must touch Him to find healing. The way we touch Him is to spend time in His presence. Ask God to heal you, and then trust Him to do it *His* way and in *His* time. Partner with God in the care of your body, knowing that, although you are the caregiver, He is the Healer.

My Prayer to God

Lord, I thank You that You are the Healer. I look to You for my healing whenever I am injured or sick. I pray that You would strengthen and heal me today. Specifically I pray for (name any area where you need the Lord to heal you). Heal me "that it might be fulfilled which was spoken by Isaiah the prophet, saying: 'He Himself took our infirmities and bore our sicknesses'" (Matthew 8:17). You suffered, died, and were buried for me so that I might have healing, forgiveness, and eternal life. By Your stripes I am healed (1 Peter 2:24). I know that in Your presence is where I will find healing. In Your presence I can reach out and touch You and in turn be touched by You.

Only You know what is best for me and what is not, so I ask that You would reveal that to me. Take away all confusing and conflicting information, and instruct me in what to eat and what to avoid. I can't do this without You, Lord, for only You know the way You created me. Give me a solid ability to be disciplined about what I eat and drink and how I exercise. Enable me to discipline my body and bring it into subjection (1 Corinthians 9:27).

Lord, You have said in Your Word, "My people are destroyed for lack of knowledge" (Hosea 4:6). I don't want to be destroyed because I lacked knowledge of the right thing to do. Teach me and help me learn. Lead me to people who can help or advise me. Enable me to follow their suggestions and directions. When I am sick and need to see a doctor, show me which doctor to see and give that doctor wisdom as to how to treat me.

The area I struggle with most in caring for my body is (name the area that presents the greatest challenge to you). Be Lord over this part of my life so that I can bring it into alignment with Your will. Help me to find freedom and deliverance in this area where it is needed.

Lord, I want everything I do to be glorifying to You. Help me to be a good steward of the body You have given me. I confess the times I have sat in judgment upon it, criticizing it in my mind for not being perfect. I repent of that and ask Your forgiveness. I know that my body is the temple of Your Holy Spirit, who dwells in me. Help me to fully understand this truth so that I will keep my temple clean and healthy. Help me not to mistreat my body in any way. Teach me how to properly care for my health.

God's Promises to Me

Is anyone among you sick? Let him call for the elders of the church, and let them pray over him, anointing him with oil in the name of the Lord. And the prayer of the faith will save the sick, and the Lord will raise him up. And if he has committed sins, he will be forgiven. Confess your trespasses to one another, and pray for one another, that you may be healed. The effective, fervent prayer of a righteous man avails much.

JAMES 5:14-16

Heal me, O LORD, and I shall be healed;
save me, and I shall be saved,
for You are my praise.
JEREMIAH 17:14

"I will restore health to you and heal you of your
wounds," says the LORD.
JEREMIAH 30:17

Therefore, whether you eat or drink,
or whatever you do, do all to the glory of God.
1 CORINTHIANS 10:31

For we know that if our earthly house, this tent, is destroyed, we have a building from God, a house not made with hands, eternal in the heavens.
2 CORINTHIANS 5:1

Chapter Twenty-Four

Lord, Free Me from Ungodly Fear

For years I couldn't take a shower without being afraid. That's because all the frightening images from the film *Psycho* kept coming back to terrify me. I had seen that film when I was young, and my shower experiences were ruined from that point on. It wasn't until I received the Lord and someone prayed for me to be delivered from fear that I was actually able to close my eyes in the shower and enjoy the water.

There were many other things I was afraid of too, such as dying, starving, failing, flying, accidents, needles, knives, getting lost, being abandoned, getting sick, being injured, the dark, the unknown, people's opinions, and being rejected. But God healed me from every one of these fears. Some I prayed about specifically. Some just went away as I learned to walk with the Lord and spend time in His love and His presence.

God does not want us to live in fear. Fear does not come from Him. It's the world that teaches us to fear. The things we see in movies, videos, newspapers, and books make us afraid. The things we hear people say and see them do causes us to have fear. The enemy can make us afraid of everything, including our future. It wears us down worrying that something we fear is going to happen. But we don't have to be tormented by fear.

Ungodly Fear

There are two kinds of fear: godly and ungodly. We must pray that we live in godly fear, which is good, and not give place to ungodly fear, which is torment. One of the most common types of ungodly fear is the fear of man, or a fear of rejection. It's a trap we can fall into without ever realizing it. In order to protect ourselves from it, we have to care more about what *God* says than what anyone else says. We must look to Him for approval and acceptance and not to people. If God does not have first place in our hearts, we are constantly fearing man. "The fear of man brings a snare, but whoever trusts in the LORD shall be safe" (Proverbs 29:25).

There are so many things to be afraid of in this world. Sometimes all it takes is one news report to fill us with fear. Our imaginations alone can frighten us. But God wants to set us free from all fear for all time.

Four Good Ways to Get Rid of Ungodly Fear

1. *Get rid of ungodly fear by praying.* The Bible says that when we are afraid it's because we have not been made perfect in love. "There is no fear in love; but perfect love casts out fear, because fear involves torment. But he who fears has not been made perfect in love" (1 John 4:18). The only love that is perfect is the love of God. The way you get perfected in His love is to draw close to Him and let Him fill you with His love. When you do, He will deliver you from all fear.

2. *Get rid of ungodly fear by controlling what you receive into your mind.* The things of the world often make us afraid.

What kind of input are you receiving from the world? Is any of it causing fear in you? How could you change that? Do you go to scary movies or watch frightening television shows? Read the Word instead. If watching the news scares you, either don't watch it or use it as a time to pray for the people and situations you hear about in it. Do whatever you can to stay close to God (for instance, you could play worship music or sing praise songs). Fear disappears in the presence of the Lord.

3. *Get rid of ungodly fear by being in the Word of God.* Many times in my life when I was afraid, I found that all fear left me just from reading the Bible. Knowing what God's Word says about our fear and the promises He has given us can make all the difference. And in the face of fear, speaking the Word out loud is a powerful weapon against it. You don't even have to be reading or speaking Scriptures specifically about fear. Reading anywhere in the Bible can take away fear, because the Spirit of the Lord can be found on every page.

4. *Get rid of ungodly fear by living in the fear of the Lord.* The more you get to know the Lord and understand who He is, the more you will reverence Him and fear His displeasure. This is called the fear of the Lord, and it makes you want to obey Him. It's what draws you closer to God and increases your longing for more of Him. It makes you forget all the things that cause you fear, because they pale in comparison to His awesome power. When you have the fear of the Lord, you fear what your life would be like without Him.

Godly Fear

Noah is a good example of godly fear. The reason he spent all that time preparing the ark for the coming flood was because he had the fear of the Lord. "By faith Noah, being divinely warned of things not yet seen, moved with godly fear, prepared an ark for the saving of his household, by which he condemned the world and became heir of the righteousness which is according to faith" (Hebrews 11:7). People laughed and made fun of him while he was building the ark, but he believed God, and he cared more about what God said than what man said. And it ended up saving his life. The best thing you can do is to "fear God and keep His commandments, for this is man's all" (Ecclesiastes 12:13). It will save your life too.

Seven Good Things That Come from Fearing God

1. *The blessing of God's provision.* "Oh, fear the LORD, you His saints! There is no want to those who fear Him" (Psalm 34:9).

2. *The blessing of God's protection.* "The fear of the Lord leads to life, and he who has it will abide in satisfaction; he will not be visited with evil" (Proverbs 19:23).

3. *The blessing of God's mercy.* "For as the heavens are high above the earth, so great is His mercy toward those who fear Him" (Psalm 103:11).

4. *The blessing of God's goodness.* "Oh, how great is Your goodness, which You have laid up for those who fear You, which You have prepared for those who trust in You in the presence of the sons of men!" (Psalm 31:19).

5. *The blessing of God's abundance.* "By humility and the fear of the LORD are riches and honor and life" (Proverbs 22:4).

6. *The blessing of God's response.* "He will fulfill the desire of those who fear Him; He also will hear their cry and save them" (Psalm 145:19).

7. *The blessing of God's freedom.* "By the fear of the LORD one departs from evil" (Proverbs 16:6).

God has secrets. It's not that He doesn't want you to know these things, it's that He wants you to get close to Him and find out. "The secret of the LORD is with those who fear Him, and He will show them His covenant" (Psalm 25:14). God wants you to walk with Him and talk with Him and have the kind of relationship with Him where He shares Himself with you and tells you things you didn't know before and wouldn't know unless He revealed them to you. When you get close enough and quiet enough, He will whisper a secret to your heart and it will change your life. In that moment, all your fear will be gone. Ask God to speak to you today.

My Prayer to God

Lord, You are my light and my salvation. You are the strength of my life. Of whom, then, shall I be afraid? Even though an entire army may surround me and go to war against me, my heart will not fear (Psalm 27:1-3). I will be strong and of good courage, for I know that You are with me wherever I go (Joshua 1:9). Free me from all ungodly fear, for I know that fear is never of You.

Guard my heart and mind from the spirit of fear. What I am afraid of today is (name anything that causes you to have fear). Take that fear and replace it with Your perfect love. If I have any thoughts in my mind that are fueled by fear, reveal them to me. If I have gotten my mind off of You and on my circumstances, help me to reverse that process so that my mind is off my circumstances and on You. Show me where I allow fear to take root and help me to put a stop to it. Take away any fear of rejection and all fear of man from within me and replace it with the fear of the Lord.

Your Word says that You will put fear in the hearts of Your people and You will not turn away from doing them good (Jeremiah 32:40). I pray that You would do that for me. I know that You have not given me a spirit of fear, so I reject that and instead claim the power, love, and sound mind You have for me. "Oh, how great is Your goodness, which You have laid up for those who fear You" (Psalm 31:19). Because I have received a kingdom which cannot be shaken, may I have grace by which to serve You acceptably with reverence and godly fear all the days of my life (Hebrews 12:28).

Thank You that "the fear of the LORD leads to life, and he who has it will abide in satisfaction; he will not be visited with evil" (Proverbs 19:23). Help me to grow in fear and reverence of You so that I may please You and escape the plans of evil for my life. Thank You that those who fear You will never lack any good thing.

God's Promises to Me

God has not given us a spirit of fear, but of power and of love and of a sound mind.

2 Timothy 1:7

There is no fear in love; but perfect love casts out fear, because fear involves torment. But he who fears has not been made perfect in love.

1 John 4:18

Teach me Your way, O LORD; I will walk in Your truth; unite my heart to fear Your name.
PSALM 86:11

Then they will call on me, but I will not answer; they will seek me diligently, but they will not find me. Because they hated knowledge and did not choose the fear of the LORD.
PROVERBS 1:28,29

Yes, if you cry out for discernment, and lift up your voice for understanding, if you seek her as silver, and search for her as for hidden treasures; then you will understand the fear of the LORD, and find the knowledge of God.
PROVERBS 2:3-5

Chapter Twenty-Five

Lord, Use Me to Touch the Lives of Others

During the months when I was writing *The Power of a Praying® Wife*, I felt led by the Holy Spirit to pray something I had never prayed before. I have always asked God to help me write every book, but this time in addition to that I felt led by the Spirit to pray that this would be a breakthrough book in terms of how many people it would reach. I had written three books previously and had never thought to pray that way. I shared what I was feeling with my prayer group, and they were in complete agreement. Together we prayed that God would take this book to the ends of the earth and see that it was translated into many other languages. I could hardly believe I was asking God for something so grand, but I felt with all my heart this was exactly the way God wanted us to pray. We prayed that prayer every week until long after the book was published.

Over the next several years, publishers from different countries around the world wrote to ask for permission to translate the book in their nation's language and publish it. Soon copies of my book arrived at my door that were translated into French, German, Portuguese, Nigerian, Indian,

Dutch, Hungarian, Korean, Spanish, Japanese, Indonesian, and Afrikaans. Each time my heart leaped with joy that God had answered my prayer so powerfully.

One day I received a box of my books that had been translated into Chinese, and I broke down and cried. It was something I never dreamed possible. I could picture all these precious Chinese women, whom I would never meet, reading this book and learning to pray for their families. There was no way I could physically travel all over the world to reach this many people in all these different countries, and I knew I would never get to China. But the message God had given me would. These people will never know me, but they will know God better.

What a powerful answer to prayer. The members of my prayer group and I have spoken many times about the first day we prayed that prayer and what God has done in response to it. Since then, with each book I have written I have prayed, "God, use me to touch the lives of others around the world with Your love, mercy, hope, and truth." You can pray that prayer too, and God will use your abilities and talents to touch others powerfully. When your heart is to give to others from what God has given to you, He will enable you to do that.

Giving to God and to other people is such a vitally important part of our life on this earth that we can never achieve all we want to see happen in our lives if we're not doing that. It's a major factor in realizing the complete purposes of God for us. We can never be truly whole and fulfilled or find any lasting peace unless we are giving to others. We release the flow of God's blessings *to* us by letting them flow *through* us. Giving to God and to others creates a vacuum into which God pours more blessings. If we stop up that flow, we stop up our lives. We must pray that God will show us how give and enable us to do it.

The Gift of Prayer

Many people have written to me and told me how my books have helped save their marriages, their children, or their lives. They asked what they could do for me in return. I always respond by saying, "The greatest thing you can do for me is to pray for me. Pray for my protection, my health, my family, and my marriage. Pray for me to have a clear mind and be able to write books that will draw people to the Lord so He can transform their lives." There is no greater gift I can receive than someone's prayers. I believe the prayers of thousands of people saved my life when I was in the hospital. If you were one of them, I am eternally grateful. I felt your prayers, and they are the reason I am alive today.

Prayer is the greatest gift we can give to anyone. Of course, if someone needs food, clothes, and a place to live, those needs must be met. But in giving that way, we can't neglect to pray for them as well. Material things are temporary, but our prayers for another person can affect them for a lifetime.

We can never move into all God has for us until we first move into intercessory prayer. This is one part of our calling that we have in common, because we are *all* called to intercede for others. God wants us to love others enough to lay down our lives for them in prayer.

On September 11, intercessors began immediately to pray for the people involved in the tragedies in New York City, Pennsylvania, and Washington, D.C. Then from all over the United States people drove to New York City because they wanted to help. They stood in line to give blood.

They gave money to bereaved families. Everyone did what they could, but it all started with prayer. "Let us not love in word or in tongue, but in deed and in truth" (1 John 3:18). If you love God, you will love people and it will motivate you to do whatever you can to help them. Prayer is a good place to start.

God wants us to give to others. He says if we don't help others in need, we don't really love Him. "But whoever has this world's goods, and sees his brother in need, and shuts up his heart from him, how does the love of God abide in him?" (1 John 3:17). "Let no one seek his own, but each one the other's well-being" (1 Corinthians 10:24). "He who has a generous eye will be blessed, for he gives of his bread to the poor" (Proverbs 22:9). The greatest blessings will come to you when you ask God to use you to touch the lives of others.

My Prayer to God

Lord, help me to serve You the way You want me to. Reveal to me any area of my life where I should be giving to someone right now. Open my eyes to see the need. Give me a generous heart to give to the poor. Help me to be a good steward of the blessings You have given me by sharing what I have with others. Show me whom You want me to extend my hand to at this time. Fill me with Your love for all people, and help me to communicate it in a way that can be clearly perceived. Use me to touch the lives of others with the hope that is in me.

Help me to give to You the way I should. I don't want to rob You of anything that is due You. Lord, I know that where my treasure is, there my heart will be also (Matthew 6:21). May my greatest treasure always be in serving You.

Lord, show me what You want me to do today to be a blessing to others around me. Specifically, show me how I can serve my family, my friends, my church, and the people whom You put in my life. I don't want to get so wrapped up in my own life that I don't see the opportunity for ministering Your life to others. Show me what You want me to do and enable me to do it. Give me all I need to minister life, hope, help, and healing to others. Make me to be one of Your faithful intercessors, and teach me how to pray in power. Help me to make a big difference in the world because You are working through me to touch the lives of others for Your glory.

God's Promises to Me

As each one has received a gift, minister it to one another, as good stewards of the manifold grace of God. If anyone speaks, let him speak as the oracles of God. If anyone ministers, let him do it as with the ability which God supplies, that in all things God may be glorified through Jesus Christ, to whom belongs the glory and the dominion forever and ever.

1 Peter 4:10-11

By this we know love, because He laid down His life for us. And we also ought to lay down our lives for the brethren.

1 John 3:16

And let us not grow weary while doing good, for in due season we shall reap if we do not lose heart.

Galatians 6:9

Those who are wise shall shine like the brightness
of the firmament, and those who turn many to
righteousness like the stars forever and ever.
DANIEL 12:3

Most assuredly, I say to you, he who believes in Me,
the works that I do he will do also; and greater works
than these he will do, because I go to My Father.
And whatever you ask in My name, that I will do,
that the Father may be glorified in the Son. If you
ask anything in My name, I will do it.
JOHN 14:12-14

CHAPTER TWENTY-SIX

Lord, Train Me to Speak Only Words That Bring Life

When I was 14, I introduced a neighbor boy to one of my girlfriends as "Fat Mike." All the other kids called him "Fat Mike" to distinguish him from the other Mikes who weren't. The moment I did that, however, I saw a hurt look in his eyes, and I realized that this was not a name *he* called himself. I felt very bad about that because I never intended to hurt him. In fact, I thought Mike was good-looking, and I didn't find his being on the heavy side as unattractive. But he obviously did. I just thought this was a funny nickname that he was okay with. He obviously wasn't. I was too ignorant at the time to realize no one feels good about a name like that. And I was also too embarrassed and immature to apologize. I hoped that by pretending the entire incident didn't happen that he would forget about it and everything would be fine.

I moved away not long after that and never saw him again. I didn't think much about that incident until about 15 years later, after I became a believer. Wanting to be completely right with God and mend the past, I asked the Lord to bring to my mind anything I needed to be forgiven of so

I could confess it to Him. My mind was flooded with many memories of things I had done wrong, and one of them was my introduction of Mike. I felt terrible about my unintentionally cruel and thoughtless words and the damage they must have done. I couldn't believe that after all the times I had been hurt in my life by the callous comments of others, I had done the same thing to someone else. I asked God to forgive me for being so unloving and stupid.

If I could have found Mike and apologized to him in person, I would have. But I couldn't, so I tried to make it up to him by praying that God would bless his life in every way. I prayed that somehow the words I said would be retracted from his memory or at least lose their sting and he would be healed of any pain my comment must have caused him. I prayed he would be able to forgive me. I prayed I could forgive myself.

One of areas that can cause the greatest trouble in our lives is located on the face between the chin and the nose. With our mouth we can say things we shouldn't and end up hurting others and paying the consequences. I was paying the consequences for words I had said 15 years ago. We can't take our words back once we speak them. All we can do is apologize and hope to be forgiven by the offended party. The best way to make sure that what comes out of our mouth is good is to put thoughts in our heart that are good. "Out of the abundance of the heart the mouth speaks" (Matthew 12:34). If we fill our heart with God's truth and God's love, that's what will come out.

Have you ever been around someone who complains all the time or speaks negatively about themselves and others? Isn't it exhausting? Have you been with the kind of person who you never knew what horrible thing might come out of their mouth? You can hardly wait to get away from them.

The Bible says we are to "do all things without complaining and disputing" (Philippians 2:14). If we complain, it reflects our lack of faith in God. It proves that we don't believe God is in charge and can take care of us. It suggests that we don't trust God will answer prayer. It shows we are not praying. Being around people with such an obvious lack of faith is depleting.

Imagine if every time we opened our mouths we spoke words that were laced with healing, edification, encouragement, comfort, wisdom, love, and truth. That's possible to do if we ask God to help us. It's dangerous to speak whatever comes into your mind—unless what comes into your mind is good. If you have your mind fixed on good things, then the words of your mouth will reflect that.

Eight Good Things to Think About Daily
(From Philippians 4:8)

1. *Whatever things are true*. If you think about what is honest, genuine, authentic, sincere, faithful, accurate, and truthful, then you won't be saying anything false, incorrect, erroneous, deceitful, or untrue.

2. *Whatever things are noble*. If you think about what is admirable, high quality, excellent, magnanimous, superior, or honorable, then you won't be saying anything that is base, petty, mean, dishonorable, or low-minded.

3. *Whatever things are just*. If you think about what is fair, reasonable, equitable, proper, lawful, right, correct, deserved, upright, honorable, and seemly, then you won't be saying anything that is unjustified, biased, unreasonable, unlawful, or unfair.

4. *Whatever things are pure*. If you think about what is clean, clear, spotless, chaste, unsullied, undefiled, or untainted with evil, then you won't be saying anything that is

inferior, tainted, adulterated, defiled, polluted, corrupted, tarnished, or unholy.

5. *Whatever things are lovely*. If you think about what is pleasing, agreeable, charming, satisfying, or splendid, then you won't be saying anything that is unpleasant, offensive, disagreeable, revolting, unlovely, ominous, or ugly.

6. *Whatever things are of good report*. If you think about what is admirable, winsome, worthwhile, recommended, positive, or worthy of repeating, then you won't be saying anything that is negative, discouraging, undesirable, or full of bad news, gossip, and rumor.

7. *Whatever things are virtuous*. If you think about what is moral, ethical, upright, excellent, good, impressive, or conforming to high moral standards, then you won't be saying anything that is depraved, unethical, licentious, bad, self-indulgent, dissipated, evil, or immoral.

8. *Whatever things are praiseworthy*. If you think about what is laudable, admirable, commendable, valuable, acclaimed, applauded, glorified, exalted, honored, or approved of, then you won't be saying anything that is critical, condemning, deprecating, disapproving, disparaging, denouncing, belittling, or depressing.

When a Wise Woman Speaks

When a wise woman speaks, she gives a reason for the hope that is within her. The most important words we can speak are ones that explain our faith to anyone who asks or who will listen. We must be able to give a reason for the hope we have within us (1 Peter 3:15). We have to pray that God will help us become bold enough to clearly explain our faith in God. We have to ask God to help us tell others why we call Jesus our Messiah, why we can't live without the Holy Spirit, and why we choose to live God's way. And we must be able to do this in a manner that is loving and humble, otherwise we will alienate those whom God wants to draw to Himself. If the love of God and the testimony of His goodness are not in our heart, then they will not come out of our mouth. And what we say will not draw people to the Lord. It may, in fact, do the exact opposite.

When a wise woman speaks, she knows that timing is important. When things need to be said that are difficult for the hearer to receive, timing is everything. Certain words cannot be uttered with any success if the person listening is not open and ready to hear them. It's important to discern that, and the only way to know for certain when to speak and what to say is to pray about it in advance. The Bible says that we are not to be too hasty to speak (Proverbs 29:20). A wise woman knows she shouldn't share every single thought that comes into her head. "A fool vents all his feelings, but a wise man holds them back" (Proverbs 29:11). You may have good things to say, but people aren't always ready to hear them. Only God knows for sure when someone is ready. Ask Him to show you.

When a wise woman speaks, she tells the truth. When we don't speak the truth, we hurt others as well as ourselves. "Therefore, putting away lying, 'Let each one of you speak the truth with his neighbor,' for we are members of one another" (Ephesians 4:25). But we can't run around speaking the truth without wisdom, sensitivity, and a sense of the Lord's timing. People don't want to hear every bit of truth about themselves every moment. It's too much for them. Sometimes it's better to say nothing and pray for God to show you when a person is ready to hear the truth.

When a wise woman speaks, she doesn't talk too much. We have to be careful that we don't spend more time talking than is necessary. "A fool's voice is known by his many words" (Ecclesiastes 5:3). I always told my prayer group that we shouldn't spend more time talking about our requests than we do praying for them. And we can't just spill words out of our mouth without giving thought to what we are saying. We will give account of every idle word in the day of judgment (Matthew 12:36). This is a very scary thought. We must ask God to make us wise in the amount of talking we do.

When a wise woman speaks, her words are gracious. We can't speak words that are mean, insensitive, harsh, coarse, rude, deceitful, offensive, or arrogant without reaping the consequences. With our words we will either build lives or we will tear them down. "Those things which proceed out of the mouth come from the heart, and they defile a man" (Matthew 15:18). "The words of a wise man's mouth are gracious, but the lips of a fool shall swallow him up" (Ecclesiastes 10:12). Ask God to create in you a clean heart so filled with His Spirit, His love, and His truth that it will overflow love, truth, and healing in your speech. Ask Him to help you find words that speak life to those around you.

My Prayer to God

Lord, help me be a person who speaks words that build up and not tear down. Help me to speak life into the situations and people around me, and not death. Fill my heart afresh each day with Your Holy Spirit so that Your love and goodness overflow from my heart and my mouth. Help me to speak only about things that are true, noble, just, pure, lovely, of good report, virtuous, and praiseworthy. "Let the words of my mouth and the meditation of my heart be acceptable in Your sight, O LORD, my strength and my Redeemer" (Psalm 19:14). Keep my mouth from speaking any evil or anything that is not true. Holy Spirit of truth, guide me in all truth. Help me to "speak as the oracles of God" and with the ability You supply so that You may be glorified (1 Peter 4:11). May every word I speak reflect Your purity and love.

Your Word says that "the preparations of the heart belong to man, but the answer of the tongue is from the LORD" (Proverbs 16:1). I will prepare my heart by being in your Word every day and obeying Your laws. I will prepare my heart by worshiping You and giving thanks in all things. Fill my heart with love, peace, and joy so that it will flow from my mouth. Convict me when I complain or speak negatively. Help me not to speak too quickly or too much. Help me not to speak words that miscommunicate. I pray You would give me the words to say every time I speak. Show me when to speak and when not to. And when I do speak, give me words to say that will bring life and edification.

Help me to be a woman who speaks wisely, graciously, and clearly and never foolishly, rudely, or insensitively. Give me words that speak of the hope that is within me so I can explain my faith in a persuasive and compelling way. May the words I speak bring others into a fuller knowledge of You.

GOD'S *PROMISES* TO ME

He who would love life and see good days,
let him refrain his tongue from evil, and his
lips from speaking deceit.

1 PETER 3:10

The heart of the wise teaches his mouth,
and adds learning to his lips.
PROVERBS 16:23

Sanctify the Lord God in your hearts, and always be ready to give a defense to everyone who asks you a reason for the hope that is in you, with meekness and fear; having a good conscience, that when they defame you as evildoers, those who revile your good conduct in Christ may be ashamed. For it is better, if it is the will of God, to suffer for doing good than for doing evil.
1 PETER 3:15-17

Pleasant words are like a honeycomb, sweetness to the soul and health to the bones.
PROVERBS 16:24

Righteous lips are the delight of kings, and they love him who speaks what is right.
PROVERBS 16:13

Chapter Twenty-Seven

Lord, Transform Me into a Woman of Mountain-Moving Faith

On my tenth birthday, I received a necklace that consisted of a small glass ball hanging from a delicate gold chain. Inside the ball was the tiniest mustard seed. I thought at the time, *Why in the world did they bother putting a seed in there that was so small it could hardly be seen*. Obviously, I didn't get the point.

It wasn't until some time later that I learned the significance of that little seed. Jesus said, "If you have faith as a mustard seed, you will say to this mountain, 'Move from here to there', and it will move; and nothing will be impossible for you" (Matthew 17:20). I've since thought a lot about how tiny that seed was. If that's all the faith it takes to move mountains, then surely I can come up with enough to move the obstacles in my life.

God takes the tiniest bit of faith we have and makes it grow into something big when we act on it. The Bible says that "God has dealt to each one a measure of faith" (Romans 12:3). We already have some faith to start with.

When we step out in that faith, God *increases* our faith. In other words, acting in faith begets more faith.

Whether you realize it or not, you are living by faith everyday. Each time you go to a doctor, you trust he will do the right thing. When you buy medicine from the pharmacist, you believe he will fill your prescription correctly. When you go to a restaurant, you have faith they will not poison you. (Some restaurants require more faith than others.) How much easier and more certain is it to trust God?

We have no idea what great things God wants to do through us if we would just step out in faith when He asks us to. That's why He lets us go through some difficult times. Times when we feel weak and vulnerable. He allows certain things to happen so that we will turn to Him and give Him our full attention. It's in those times, when we are forced to pray in greater faith, that our faith grows stronger.

Jesus said, "According to your faith let it be to you" (Matthew 9:29). This could be a frightening thought, depending on the kind of faith you have. But there are things we can do to increase our faith, such as read the Word of God. Faith comes by simply hearing it (Romans 10:17). When you take the promises and truths in His Word and declare them out loud, you'll sense your faith increasing.

Praying increases our faith as well because it's how we reach out and touch God. At one point a woman reached out to the Lord believing that if she just "touched the hem of His garment" she could be healed. Jesus told her that her faith had made her well, and she was healed at that very time (Matthew 9:20-22). Every time we reach out and touch Him in prayer, our lives are healed in some way and our faith is increased.

Every day it becomes more and more crucial that we have faith. There will be times in each of our lives when we will need the kind of faith that makes the difference between success or failure, winning or losing, life or death. That's why asking for more faith must be an ongoing prayer. No matter how much faith you have, God can increase it.

Even when your faith seems small, you can still speak in faith to the mountains in your life and tell them to move, and God will do the impossible. You can pray for the crippled parts of your life to be healed and God will restore them. You can ask God to increase your faith and give you boldness to act on it, and He will do it.

What promise of God would you like to claim in faith as your own right now? What prayer would you like to boldly pray in faith and see answered? What would you like to see accomplished in your life, or in the life of someone you know, that would take a prayer of great faith? Ask God to take that seed you have and grow it into a giant tree of faith so you can see these things come to pass.

My Prayer to God

Lord, increase my faith. Teach me how to "walk by faith, not by sight" (2 Corinthians 5:7). Give me strength to stand strong on Your promises and believe Your every word. I don't want to be like the people who did not profit from hearing the Word because it wasn't mixed with faith (Hebrews 4:2). I know that "faith comes by hearing, and hearing by the word of God" (Romans 10:17). Make my faith increase every time I hear or read Your Word. Help me to believe for Your promises to be fulfilled in me. I pray that the genuineness of my faith, which is more precious than gold that perishes even when it is tested by fire, will be glorifying to You, Lord (1 Peter 1:7).

I know "faith is the substance of things hoped for, the evidence of things not seen" (Hebrews 11:1). I know I have been "saved through faith," and it is a gift from You (Ephesians 2:8). Increase my faith so that I can pray in power. Give me faith to believe for healing every time I pray for the sick. I don't want to see a need and then not have faith strong enough to pray and believe for the situation to change.

Help me to take the "shield of faith" to "quench all the fiery darts of the wicked one" (Ephesians 6:16). Help me "to ask in faith, with no doubting." For I know that "he who doubts is like a wave of the sea driven and tossed by the wind." I know that a doubter is double-minded and unstable and will not receive anything from You (James 1:6-8). I know that "whatever is not from faith is sin" (Romans 14:23). I confess any doubt I have as sin before You, and I ask You to forgive me. I don't want to hinder what You want to do in me and through me because of doubt. Increase my faith daily so that I can move mountains in Your name.

God's Promises to Me

Without faith it is impossible to please Him, for he who comes to God must believe that He is, and that He is a rewarder of those who diligently seek Him.

Hebrews 11:6

All things are possible to him who believes.
MARK 9:23

If you have faith as a mustard seed, you will say to this mountain, "Move from here to there," and it will move; and nothing will be impossible for you.
MATTHEW 17:20

Having been justified by faith, we have peace with God through our Lord Jesus Christ.
ROMANS 5:1

In this you greatly rejoice, though now for a little while, if need be, you have been grieved by various trials, that the genuineness of your faith, being much more precious than gold that perishes, though it is tested by fire, may be found to praise, honor, and glory at the revelation of Jesus Christ.
1 PETER 1:6-7

CHAPTER TWENTY-EIGHT

Lord, Change Me into the Likeness of Christ

I recently heard a pastor speak about his experience as a missionary starting a church in a remote part of the world. He told how when he and his wife first arrived at the little village where they were going to plant this new church, they were shocked at how little the native people of that region wore in the way of clothing. It was a hot and humid land, so the men and women only wore strips of cloth that covered the area between their waist and mid-thigh. The women were completely topless. The first thing the pastor and his wife did was to instruct the ladies that they needed to be covered on top. In order to help them do that, the pastor sent for T-shirts to be delivered to the village.

When the shirts arrived, one was given to each woman. They were very excited to receive them and eagerly took them home, promising to wear them when they came back. The next day when everyone gathered together again, the pastor and his wife were even more shocked than before. Each woman had taken her shirt and cut two large round holes out of the front of it so that when they put the shirts on, their breasts stuck through the holes.

I laughed when I heard that story and wondered how many times God gives us something to cover us or to make us right with Him, and we cut out the part that we don't want so that our flesh can still stick through.

No wonder we aren't able change ourselves. We don't even understand what we're supposed to be changed to or why. Only God can open our eyes to see these things. That's why we have to pray the "Change me, Lord" prayer. I know it's one of the most frightening and difficult prayers to pray. We'd so much rather pray, "Change *him*, Lord" or "Change *her*, Lord." Plus if we give the Lord *carte blanche* to do whatever He wants in us, God only knows what He might do.

But there is a way we can pray that will change us, and it's not frightening. That is to pray, "Make me more like Christ." Who doesn't want to exhibit the character of Jesus? Who doesn't want to be more like Him in every way?

Seven Good Ways to Be More Like Christ

1. *Jesus was loving.* Not only was Jesus loving, but His love was beyond comprehension. We will never have to bear the sin of the world unto death the way He did, but He wants us to lay down our lives for people in other ways. "By this we know love, because He laid down His life for us. And we also ought to lay down our lives for the brethren" (1 John 3:16). His love can work miracles in your life and in the lives of people you touch. The love of God in you will grow and reproduce as you share it. "A new commandment I give to you, that you love one another; as I have loved you, that you also love one another" (John 13:34). Pray for God's love to be revealed in you as you reach out to the world around you.

2. *Jesus was humble*. Jesus was Lord of the universe, yet "He humbled Himself and became obedient to the point of death, even the death of the cross" (Philippians 2:8). Even a fraction of His humility will get us a long way in this world, because it's such a rare commodity. And we need it because there is a steep price to pay for having pride. "Everyone proud in heart is an abomination to the LORD; though they join forces, none will go unpunished" (Proverbs 16:5). "Pride goes before destruction, and a haughty spirit before a fall" (Proverbs 16:18). Nothing will speak louder to people around you than your own humility, because it will be a refreshing departure from the norm. Pray for God to give you a humble heart.

3. *Jesus was faithful*. Jesus never wavered in His conviction and knowledge of who He was and why He was on earth. "I am the way, the truth, and the life. No one comes to the Father except through Me" (John 14:6). Even when He was tempted by Satan, He never faltered. We need to know with that same certainty who *He* really is, so we can know who *we* really are. Then we won't waver. Ask God to strengthen your inner being and make you as faithful as He is.

4. *Jesus was giving*. Jesus gave of Himself to disciple a few men so that many lives would be touched. He gave of His power so that many would be healed, delivered, and made whole. "If I then, your Lord and Teacher, have washed your feet, you also ought to wash one another's feet. For I have given you an example, that you should do as I have done to you" (John 13:14-15). His ultimate gift was His life. "Christ also suffered for us, leaving us an example, that you should follow His steps" (1 Peter 2:21). When we don't feel we have anything to give, God supplies it all. "God is able to make all grace abound toward you, that you, always having

all sufficiency in all things, may have an abundance for every good work" (2 Corinthians 9:8). Pray that God will fill you with His good gifts to give to those He brings into your life.

5. *Jesus was separate*. Jesus was *in* the world, but He was not a *part of* the world. He came to *touch* the world, but He never became *like* the world. He was separate from the world, yet He changed the world around Him. We must pray that we can find that balance too. We can't stay so separate that we have no touch with the outside world. Nor can we be looking, living, talking, and acting so much like the world that people don't see anything different about us. Jesus never lost sight of where He was going. He always kept eternity in His perspective. We must do the same. Pray that you will always remember who you are, what you are called to do, and where you are going to spend eternity.

6. *Jesus was obedient*. One of the most amazing things about Jesus was that even though He was Lord, He still did not do anything on His own. He prayed and did not act until He had instructions from God. We must live that way too. "He who says he abides in Him ought himself also to walk just as He walked" (1 John 2:6). Jesus was obedient to the point of death. Can there be any greater level of obedience? He did what He had to do because He knew the great things that would come out of it. We have to do the same, "looking unto Jesus, the author and finisher of our faith, who for the joy that was set before Him endured the cross, despising the shame, and has sat down at the right hand of the throne of God. For consider Him who endured such hostility from sinners against Himself, lest you become weary and discouraged in your souls" (Hebrews 12:2-3). Ask God to help you die to yourself so that you can live for Him.

7. *Jesus was light.* People are drawn to light. We want them to be drawn to the light of the Lord in us. Jesus said, "I am the light of the world. He who follows Me shall not walk in darkness, but have the light of life" (John 8:12). We don't want to walk in the dark. We want to be in the light as He is in the light. Ask God to make you more like Christ so that everyplace you go people will stop you and say, "Tell me what you know." "What is this special thing you have?" "What must I do to get what you've got?" And you will be able to give them the reason for the light within you.

My Prayer to God

Lord, I want to be changed, and I pray those changes will begin today. I know I can't change myself in any way that is significant or lasting, but by the transforming power of Your Holy Spirit all things are possible. Grant me, according to the riches of Your glory, to be strengthened with might through Your Spirit in my inner being (Ephesians 3:16). Transform me into Your likeness. I know that You will supply all that I need according to Your riches in Christ Jesus (Philippians 4:19).

Help me to become separate from the world without becoming isolated from it or turning my back on it. Show me when I am not humble and help me to resist pride of any kind. Let my humility be a testimony of Your Spirit in me. May Your love manifested in me be a witness of Your greatness. Teach me to love others the way You do.

Soften my heart where it has become hard. Make me fresh where I have become stale. Lead me and instruct me where I have become unteachable. Make me to be faithful, giving, and obedient the way Jesus was. Where I am resistant to change, help me to trust Your work in my life. May Your light so shine in me that I become a light to all who know me. May it be not I who lives, but You who lives in me (Galatians 2:20). Make me to be so much like Christ that when people see me they will want to know You better.

God's Promises to Me

I have been crucified with Christ; it is no longer I who live, but Christ lives in me; and the life which I now live in the flesh I live by faith in the Son of God, who loved me and gave Himself for me.
Galatians 2:20

The Spirit Himself bears witness with our spirit that we are children of God, and if children, then heirs—heirs of God and joint heirs with Christ, if indeed we suffer with Him, that we may also be glorified together.
Romans 8:16-17

Come out from among them and be separate, says the Lord. Do not touch what is unclean, and I will receive you. I will be a Father to you, and you shall be my sons and daughters, says the Lord Almighty.
2 Corinthians 6:17-18

My grace is sufficient for you, for My strength is made perfect in weakness. Therefore most gladly I will rather boast in my infirmities, that the power of Christ may rest upon me.
2 Corinthians 12:9

I can do all things through Christ who strengthens me.
Philippians 4:13

Chapter Twenty-Nine

Lord, Lift Me out of My Past

Imagine that you are running in a race, and you're trying to reach the goal and ultimately win the prize. But as hard as you try you can never get to the finish line because there is a heavy weight tied around one of your legs. You struggle to pull it along, but it slows you down and causes you to be so weary and exhausted that you are tempted to give up altogether. It doesn't occur to you that this is something you don't have to carry. It has been so much a part of you for so long that you never imagined life without it. Yet you can't finish the race and secure the prize God has for you until you become free of it.

This scenario is true for so many of us. We are trying to run the race of life, but we are having trouble getting up to speed. That's because we've been carrying excess baggage from the past around with us without even realizing it. In fact, we've carried it around with us for so long we think it's part of us. Some days are so hard we feel like giving up and getting out of the race. But I have good news. God wants to take that burden from you so you will never have to carry it again.

Whether it's something that happened as long ago as your early childhood or as recently as yesterday, the past can keep you from moving into all God has for you. That's why He wants to set you free from it. And not only that, He wants to redeem and restore what has been lost or destroyed in your past and make it count for something important in your life now. The truth is, you can never move into the future God has for you if you are continually stuck in the past. When you received Jesus you became a new creation. He made *all* things new in your life, and He wants you to live like it.

God says to forget the former things, but that's not easy to do. How do we forget what happened to us? Do we need to have amnesia? Or a frontal lobotomy? Must we live in denial? Do we have to pretend that the past did not happen? Should we have part of our brain liposuctioned? The answer is no to all of the above. We just have to pray that God will set us free from the past so we can live successfully in the present.

One of the great mysteries of the Lord is how He can take the horrible, the tragic, the painful, the devastating, the embarrassing, and the ruinous experiences and memories of our lives and not only heal them, but use them for good. It's not that He will make you unable to recall them, but He will heal you so thoroughly from their effects that you no longer think about them with any pain. He will give you a new life you enjoy so much you don't want to travel back in your mind to the old one. You will still have the memory, but you no longer have the pain. Instead, you will have praise in your heart for the way God has restored you to wholeness. And you will want to share your experience with others so that they can know this kind of deliverance, restoration, and healing is there for them too.

Intended for Good

The reason God doesn't want to wipe your past completely out of your memory is because He wants to use that part of your life for the work He has called you to do. He can take the worst thing about your past and make it to be your greatest blessing in the future. He will weave it into the foundation of your ministry to the world, and out of it you will bring the life of the Lord to other people.

That's why God wants you to learn from the past and witness firsthand how He can redeem it, but He doesn't want you living there. He wants you to read your past like a history book, but not like a prophecy for your future. He wants you to forget those things that are behind you and reach forward to those things which are ahead (Philippians 3:13).

Many people never get to the future God has for them because they are perpetually stuck in the past. A good example of this are people who have experienced rejection in their past and still fear being rejected now. They expect to be rejected, so they read rejection into other people's words and actions. This causes them to always be hurt, afraid, angry, or bitter, and it makes them oversensitive to other people's comments. In other words, their *fear* of rejection *causes* the very rejection they feared. It becomes an endless cycle.

Whatever weight from the past you are carrying will be observed by others, even if they don't know what it is. The bad things that happened to us, or the good things that *didn't* happen to us, will be part of what we wear daily and people will see the total look even if they can't recall the specific details. But God will deliver you from your past and use it for His glory if you ask Him to.

Don't Look Back

Once you step out of the past it's important you don't keep looking over your shoulder to see if it's following you. That's what Lot's wife did, and it paralyzed her. It will paralyze you too. And it will definitely slow you down in the race. Good runners look forward and keep focused on the goal.

Even if you have never had one bad thing happen to you in your life, or you have been completely delivered from every negative memory you ever had, you still need to pray to be free of your past. That's because even the good things of your past can keep you from allowing God to do a new thing now. If we get locked into what we did before, we may miss what God wants to do now. God is always wanting to take you to a new place in your life, and you will keep Him from doing that if you are hanging on to the way things have always been done. He will never allow us to rest on past success. If we rely on the way things have always been done, we aren't relying on Him. And that's the whole point.

I guarantee that no matter how old you are, God has something new He wants to do in your life. Ask Him to show you what that is. Tell Him you intend to stay in the race and you don't want to carry any baggage from the past around with you. Tell Him you want to run in such a way so that you will obtain the prize (1 Corinthians 9:24).

My Prayer to God

Lord, I pray that You would set me free from my past. Wherever I have made the past my home I pray that You would deliver me, heal me, and redeem me from it. I choose to make my home with You. Help me to let go of anything I have held onto of my past that has kept me from moving into all You have for me. Enable me to put off all former ways of thinking and feeling and remembering (Ephesians 4:22-24). Give me the mind of Christ so I will be able to understand when I am being controlled by memories of past events.

I don't want to tie myself to the past by neglecting to forgive any person or event associated with it. Help me to forgive what needs to be forgiven. Specifically, I pray that You would deliver me from the effects of (name any painful or bad memory you have). I release my past to You and everyone associated with it so You can restore what has been lost. Everything that was done to me or I have done which causes me pain, I surrender to You. May it no longer torment me or affect what I do today. Make me glad according to the days in which I have been afflicted and the years I have seen evil (Psalm 90:15). Thank You that You make all things new and You are making me new in every way (Revelation 21:5).

Help me to keep my eyes looking straight ahead and not back on the former days and old ways of doing things. I know You want to do something new in my life today. Help me to concentrate on where I am to go now and not where I have been. Release me from the past so I can move out of it and into the future You have for me.

GOD'S PROMISES TO ME

If anyone is in Christ, He is a new creation;
old things have passed away; behold all
things have become new.
2 CORINTHIANS 5:17

Do not remember the former things, nor consider the
things of old. Behold, I will do a new thing,
now it shall spring forth; shall you not know it?
I will even make a road in the wilderness
and rivers in the desert.
ISAIAH 43:18-19

Brethren, I do not count myself to have apprehended; but one thing I do, forgetting those
things which are behind and reaching forward to
those things which are ahead, I press toward
the goal for the prize of the upward call
of God in Christ Jesus.
PHILIPPIANS 3:13-14

Let your eyes look straight ahead, and your eyelids
look right before you. Ponder the path of your feet,
and let all your ways be established.
Do not turn to the right or the left;
remove your foot from evil.
PROVERBS 4:25-27

God will wipe away every tear from their eyes;
there shall be no more death,
nor sorrow, nor crying. There shall be no more pain,
for the former things have passed away.
REVELATION 21:4

CHAPTER THIRTY

Lord, Lead Me into the Future You Have for Me

I'm writing this chapter as a letter to you personally, my dear sister in Christ, so that if you become anxious about your future, or you need encouragement about what is ahead, you can read it and hopefully hear God speak to your heart. For this is really His message to all of us.

Dear____________________(please fill in your name),

I am writing this because I want to remind you of the great future God has for you. I know this because He said so. He says you have not seen, nor heard, nor have even imagined anything as great as what He has prepared for you (1 Corinthians 2:9). You have no idea how great your future is. He says that what He has for you is so great that if you truly understood it, you would feel "that the sufferings of this present time are not worthy to be compared with the glory which shall be revealed" in you (Romans 8:18). That means whatever you envision for your life right now is already too small.

Although God promises you a future full of hope and blessing, it's not going to happen automatically. There are some things *you* have to do. One of them is pray about it (Jeremiah 29:11-13). Another is obey God. But don't worry, God will help you with both of those if you ask Him. The Holy Spirit is God's guarantee to you that He will help you do what you need to do and bring to pass everything He promised (Ephesians 1:13-14). Just know that every time you pray and obey, you are investing in your future.

Although we live in a world where everything in our lives can change in an instant, and we can't be certain what tomorrow will bring, God is unchanging. You may already have lost your false sense of security, and this is good because God wants you to know that your only *real* security is found in Him. Although you may not know the specific details about what is ahead, you can trust that God knows. And He will get you safely where you need to go. In fact, the way to get to the future God has for you is to walk with Him today.

Remember, my precious sister in the Lord, that walking with God doesn't mean there won't be obstacles. Satan will see to it that there are. While God has a plan for your future that is good, the devil has one too and it's not good. But the devil's plan for your life cannot succeed as long as you are walking with God, living in obedience to His ways, worshiping only Him, standing strong in His Word, and praying without ceasing. God's plan for your life won't happen without a struggle, however, so don't give up when times get tough. Just keep on doing what's right and resist the temptation to quit. Ask God to give you the strength and endurance you need to do what you have to do.

Don't judge your future by what you read in the newspapers or the words someone spoke over you one time. Your future is in *God's* hands. The only thing that is important is what *He* says about it. He doesn't want you to be concerned about your future anyway. He wants you to be concerned with *Him*, because *He* is your future.

Remember that you are God's daughter and He loves you. As you *walk* with Him, you will become more like Him every day (1 John 3:1-3). As you *look* to Him, you will be "transformed into the same image from glory to glory, just as by the Spirit of the Lord" (2 Corinthians 3:18). As you *live* with Him, He will take you from strength to strength. So even though your "outward man is perishing, yet the inward man is being renewed day by day" (2 Corinthians 4:16).

Don't become discouraged if things don't happen as fast as you would like them to. They never do. God wants you to learn patience. Our perspective is temporal. His is eternal. So don't be concerned if you are not seeing all that you want in response to your prayers. You will. If you draw close to God and do what He asks you to do, if you worship Him in spirit and in truth, if you love others and give of yourself to them, if you speak God's Word in faith and pray, you will see God's blessings poured out on your life.

I believe that we are denied certain things for a time because God wants us to fervently pray and intercede for them. That's because He wants to do something great in response to our prayers, something that can *only* be birthed in prayer. Do you remember how Hannah prayed long and fervently for a child (1 Samuel 1:1-28)? When God finally answered her prayer, it wasn't just any child who was born. Samuel was one of the world's greatest prophets and most influential judges in Israel's history. If she had not prayed so fervently, that might not have happened. There may be things that won't happen in your life unless you are praying that long and fervently too.

If you start being consumed by the details of life, and it feels as if your future won't ever be any different than it is at this moment, please know the truth is quite the opposite. It's at these very times, when you feel as though you're not getting anywhere, or you're missing the future God has for you, that God is actually *preparing* you for your future. And when the time is right, He has been known to do a very quick work. While it's good to set goals, don't look so far ahead that you become overwhelmed. Look to the Lord instead. Remember that "the Lord is near to all who call upon Him, to all who call upon Him in truth. He will fulfill the desire of those who fear Him; He also will hear their cry and save them" (Psalm 145:18-19).

One day you will be with God in heaven. And He will wipe away every tear from your eyes and "there shall be no more death, nor sorrow, nor crying. There shall be no more pain, for the former things have passed away" (Revelation 21:4). You want to be able to reach the end of your life and say, "I have fought the good fight, I have finished the race, I have kept the faith. Finally, there is laid up for me the crown of righteousness, which the Lord, the righteous Judge, will give to me on that Day, and not to me only but also to all who have loved His appearing" (2 Timothy 4:7-8). Jesus said, "Let not your heart be troubled; you believe in God, believe also in Me. In My Father's house are many mansions; if it were not so, I would have told you. I go to prepare a place for you. And if I go and prepare a place for you, I will come again and receive you to Myself; that where I am, there you may be also" (John 14:1-3). He promises that because you love Him, your eternal future in heaven with Him is secure.

In the meantime I know that you want to do something significant for the Lord and move into new areas of service for Him. God is looking for women who will be committed to living His way and stepping into the purposes He has for their lives. He wants a woman who is willing to sacrifice herself for His kingdom, who is willing to say, "Not my will, but Yours be done." You are one of those women. I pray that you will be equipped and ready when God says, "Now is the time," and the doors of opportunity open. Just keep doing what's right and when you least expect it, you will get a call from God giving you your assignment.

Remember, God "is able to do exceedingly abundantly above all that we ask or think, according to the power that works in us" (Ephesians 3:20). He has more for you than you can imagine. And now may "the God of hope fill you with all joy and peace in believing, that you may abound in hope by the power of the Holy Spirit" (Romans 15:13). Stay focused on God, and He will keep you in perfect peace as He moves you into the future He has for you.

Your sister in Christ,
Stormie Omartian

My Prayer to God

Lord, I put my future in Your hands and ask that You would give me total peace about it. I don't want to be trying to secure my future with my own plans. I want to be in the center of *Your* plans, knowing that You have given me everything I need for what is ahead. I pray You would give me strength to endure without giving up. You have said that "he who endures to the end will be saved" (Matthew 10:22). Help me to run the race in a way that I shall finish strong and receive the prize You have for me (1 Corinthians 9:24). Help me to be always watchful in my prayers, because I don't know when the end of my life will be (1 Peter 4:7).

I know Your thoughts toward me are of peace, to give me a future and a hope (Jeremiah 29:11). I know that You have saved me and called me with a holy calling, not according to my works, but according to Your own purpose and grace (2 Timothy 1:9). Thank You, Holy Spirit, that You are always with me and will guide me on the path so that I won't lose my way.

Move me into powerful ministry that will impact the lives of others for Your kingdom and Your glory. I humble myself under Your mighty hand, O God, knowing that You will lift me up in due time. I cast all my care upon You, knowing that You care for me and will not let me fall (1 Peter 5:6-7). I reach out for Your hand today so I can walk with You into the future You have for me.

GOD'S PROMISES TO ME

I know the thoughts I think toward you, says the LORD, thoughts of peace and not of evil, to give you a future and a hope. Then you will call on Me and go and pray to Me, and I will listen to you. And you will seek Me and find Me, when you search for me with all your heart.

JEREMIAH 29:11-13

Those who are planted in the house of the LORD shall flourish in the courts of our God. They shall still bear fruit in old age; they shall be fresh and flourishing, to declare that the LORD is upright.

PSALM 92:13-15

I am persuaded that neither death nor life, nor angels nor principalities nor powers, nor things present nor things to come, nor height nor depth, nor any other created thing, shall be able to separate us from the love of God which is in Christ Jesus our Lord.

ROMANS 8:38-39

But the path of the just is like the shining sun, that shines ever brighter unto the perfect day.

PROVERBS 4:18

Arise, shine; for your light has come! And the glory of the LORD is risen upon you. For behold, the darkness shall cover the earth, and deep darkness the people; but the LORD will arise over you, and His glory will be seen upon you.

ISAIAH 60:1-2

Other Books by Stormie Omartian

THE POWER OF A PRAYING® WIFE
Stormie shares how wives can develop a deeper relationship with their husbands by praying for them. With this practical advice on praying for specific areas, including decision-making, fears, spiritual strength, and sexuality, women will discover the fulfilling marriage God intended.

THE POWER OF A PRAYING® HUSBAND
Building on the success of *The Power of a Praying® Wife*, Stormie offers this guide to help husbands pray more effectively for their wives. Each chapter features comments from well-known Christian men, biblical wisdom, and prayer ideas.

THE POWER OF A PRAYING® PARENT
This powerful book for parents offers 30 easy-to-read chapters that focus on specific areas of prayers for children. This personal, practical guide leads the way to enriched, strong prayer lives for both moms and dads.

THE POWER OF A PRAYING® NATION
Learn to intercede in practical ways for our political leaders, military personnel, teachers, and those who work in the media. Affect the strength and spiritual life of our nation through prayer.

JUST ENOUGH LIGHT FOR THE STEP I'M ON
New Christians and those experiencing life changes or difficult times will appreciate Stormie's honesty, candor, and advice based on experience and the Word of God in this collection of devotional readings perfect for the pressures of today's world.

John McNichol's
Books